SPOOKY
Yellowstone

Also in the Spooky Series by
S. E. Schlosser and Paul G. Hoffman:

SPOOKY
Yellowstone

Tales of Hauntings, Strange Happenings,
and Other Local Lore

RETOLD BY S. E. SCHLOSSER

ILLUSTRATED BY PAUL G. HOFFMAN

gpp

Guilford, Connecticut

Text copyright © 2013 by S. E. Schlosser
Illustrations copyright © 2013 by Paul G. Hoffman

Editor: Meredith Dias
Project editor: Lauren Szalkiewicz
Layout: Justin Marciano
Text design: Lisa Reneson, Two Sisters Design
Map: Alena Joy Pearce © Morris Book Publishing, LLC

Library of Congress Cataloging-in-Publication Data

Schlosser, S. E.
 Spooky Yellowstone : tales of hauntings, strange happenings, and other
local lore / retold by S.E. Schlosser ; illustrated by Paul G. Hoffman.
— First [edition].
    pages cm
  ISBN 978-0-7627-8146-1
1. Haunted places—Yellowstone National Park. 2. Ghosts—Yellowstone
National Park. 3. Yellowstone National Park—Miscellanea. I. Title.
 BF1472.U6S3367 2013
 398.209787'52—dc23
                                                              2012050288

Printed in the United States of America

10 9 8 7 6 5 4 3 2 1

For my family: David, Dena, Tim, Arlene, Hannah, Emma, Nathan, Ben, Deb, Gabe, Clare, Jack, Chris, Karen, Davey, and Aunt Mil.

For Barbara and Peggy, excellent neighbors and wonderful friends. Thank you both from all of the Schlosser clan.

For Erin Turner, Paul Hoffman, and all the wonderful folks at Globe Pequot Press, with my thanks.

For Debbie Garlicki and Joel Bieler, who joined me on my Trout Lake hike and for Wim, Doug, Amy, Alicia, and Helga, who guided me on various tours through Yellowstone during my research trip.

For Petra of Cowboy Village.

For the staff of Heart Six in Moran, Wyoming, with special thanks to Laura, Karley, Whitney, Josh, Eric, Becky, Seth, Roger, Paul, and Nancy. Thank you for making my stay at the ranch so enjoyable!

Contents

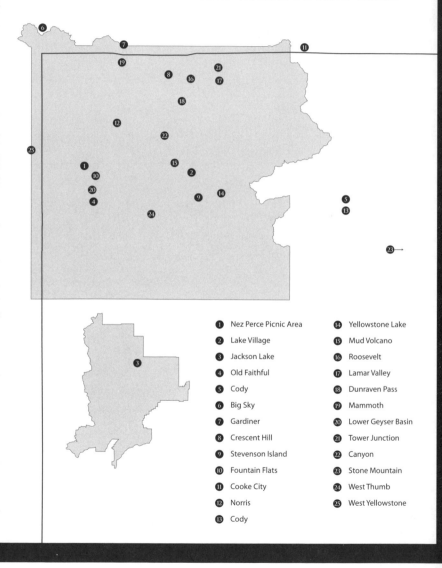

SPOOKY SITES . . .   AND WHERE TO FIND THEM

1. Nez Perce Picnic Area
2. Lake Village
3. Jackson Lake
4. Old Faithful
5. Cody
6. Big Sky
7. Gardiner
8. Crescent Hill
9. Stevenson Island
10. Fountain Flats
11. Cooke City
12. Norris
13. Cody
14. Yellowstone Lake
15. Mud Volcano
16. Roosevelt
17. Lamar Valley
18. Dunraven Pass
19. Mammoth
20. Lower Geyser Basin
21. Tower Junction
22. Canyon
23. Stone Mountain
24. West Thumb
25. West Yellowstone

Contents

Introduction

Shivers ran down my spine when the bull elk threw back his antlered head and bugled a challenge to his enemy. The young male he confronted was no match for this massive fellow. As the bull elk charged, the younger beast trotted briskly away, abandoning the females he'd meticulously gathered together a short time before. Around me, tourists exclaimed in awe and snapped pictures as the triumphant bull elk chivvied his new harem into the woods by the lake.

It was my last day in Yellowstone, and this elk sighting capped everything I'd seen up 'til now. And I'd seen some amazing things. Bison peered through my car window. Wolves howled from their den in Lamar Valley. Grand Geyser erupted so dramatically that visitors "oohed" and "ahhed" as if viewing fireworks. A pine marten darted through the underbrush while I was hiking to Storm Point with a ranger. A mama grizzly and two cubs meandered across the street in the Grand Tetons. A thunderstorm rolled through the Firehole and threw hailstones at my tour group. A moose stood scratching its back in the middle of the river, oblivious to the traffic jam it caused on the bridge.

Yellowstone was amazing! Yellowstone was terrifying. Slip into one of the lovely, colorful pools in the Geyser Basins and you were cooked. Literally. Yet the beauty of Yellowstone

captured my imagination as no other place I've seen. Mud pots, fumaroles, geysers, hot springs—where else can you find so many volcanic features in one region? Of course, they come with many dangers, some of them unseen ("The Death Pit"). And wandering alone in Yellowstone ain't no picnic, as Truman Everts could testify when he became separated from the Washburn Expedition in 1870 ("Thirty-Seven Days"). Even tough old trappers like Jim Bridger walked carefully when exploring this "Wonderland" ("Not Far Below"). Add ghost sightings to the mix of dangerous beasts and life-threatening volcanic features and the Yellowstone region may truly be classified as a Very Spooky Place.

During my visit, I collected many ghostly tales. A phantom haunts beautiful Stevenson Island in Yellowstone Lake ("The Drowned Man"). A ghost train pulls into the long-gone station at Cinnabar ("Ghost Train"). A long-dead couple wanders the bank of the Firehole River ("Mattie"). And the spirit of Buffalo Bill Cody himself haunts the Irma Hotel in the town that bears his name ("Hello, Darlin'").

By far my favorite story is the tale of a bridegroom who was chased by wolves on the way to his wedding ("The Hero of Stone Mountain"). And the most heart-wrenching was the story of a family who brought their daughter to Yellowstone, hoping to save her from herself ("Shattered").

Introduction

Yellowstone moved me deeply. America's first national park has a special place in my heart. I hope you enjoy these stories from the land where the deer and the antelope still play.

—Sandy Schlosser

PART ONE
Ghost Stories

1

Mattie

I'd lost track of time. As usual. I'd spent the morning roaming the boardwalks of Yellowstone's famous Fountain Paint Pots, taking snapshots of fabulous volcanic features: bubbling mud pots in unique colors, hissing fumaroles with hot steam puffing out of them like dragon's breath, boiling hot pools of a deadly-but-serene-looking two-hundred-degree Caribbean blue, and gushing geysers spouting water high into the air. It was enough to distract me from the basics of human existence—like my current need, discovered shortly after I turned my car north toward Madison Junction, for a ladies' room. I seriously had to *go*. There was no delicate way of phrasing it.

My biological need pressed with some urgency. If I did not find a ladies' room soon, I would have to use a bush by the roadside. Unfortunately, I appeared to be driving through a meadow at the moment. There were some interesting volcanic features steaming off to my left, but no conveniently concealing shrubbery.

Then I saw a sign for Fountain Flat Drive and—eureka!— what looked like a picnic area, which might have a primitive restroom. Or a bush. I hung a left, then a quick right, and parked the car with impressive speed. Levitating out of the driver's seat,

I hurtled toward a brown building with a restroom sign, my feet barely touching the pavement.

I emerged a few minutes later in a much happier frame of mind, scrubbing sanitizer onto my hands as I looked around with renewed interest. The Nez Perce Picnic Area stood between two bodies of water, a small creek on my right and the Firehole River on my left. This was a nice spot to have lunch, I decided, and headed to the car for my picnic basket. The sun glittered enticingly upon the Firehole River, so I made my way through the evergreens and sagebrush, choosing a picnic table near the riverbank. I unpacked my lunch upon the weathered-gray table while a Clark's nutcracker called sassily from a nearby branch, eyeing the food with interest.

"This food is mine, not yours," I informed the bird as I unpacked tuna salad, trail mix, a bag of chips, and a soda. "According to park regulations, tourists are supposed to stay twenty-five yards away from wildlife. This means you!"

Ignoring park regulations, the bird launched itself from the branch and perched on a nearby table. "I may have to report you to a ranger," I threatened as I settled down to eat. The nutcracker chirruped beguilingly, its eyes fixed on my food.

My conversation with the bird was interrupted when a soft voice behind me said, "Do you mind if I join you?"

I jumped about a mile, nearly spilling my soda. I hadn't heard footsteps or seen anyone nearby. Where had this stranger come from? There was no place to hide among the low-growing sagebrush and golden meadow grass.

I whirled in my seat to look at the stranger. It was a woman in an old-fashioned long dress with a long coat buttoned over it. She wore a smashing hat that I rather envied, and she looked

MATTIE

chilled—rather surprising in this warm sunshine. I wondered if she was a Mennonite or one of the other faiths that require traditional dress for their congregation.

"Good afternoon," I said belatedly, returning the woman's smile. "Please, join me." I gestured at the bench beside me.

The woman gracefully took a seat, long dress swishing around her. "My name is Mattie," she said.

"I'm Karen," I replied.

"Are you staying at the Firehole Hotel?" she asked.

I'd never heard of the Firehole Hotel, but I wasn't familiar with all the amenities in Yellowstone. I'd mostly paid attention to the places I could park my little camper.

"I'm camping up at Madison," I said. "Are you staying at the hotel?"

"My husband has a job with the Yellowstone Park Association. They've provided us with a place at the hotel," Mattie said.

I sighed with envy. "It must be wonderful to work here," I said. "I love the wild beauty of this place. And you can't beat the view!" I gestured to the sparkling river flowing through the wide, grassy meadow, framed by the pine-covered mountains. The sagebrush added some green to the seared yellow grass, and the rapids burbled soft background music to the birds chirping.

Mattie coughed, a deep hacking sound. "I beg your pardon," she apologized as she wiped her mouth with a lace handkerchief. Somewhat restored to herself, she continued, "We love it here. My little girl, Theda, loves the animals. One of her first words was 'bison.'"

"How old is Theda?" I asked, taking a bite of sandwich. I offered Mattie some of my trail mix, but she shook her head.

"Theda turned a year in June," Mattie replied. "She doesn't remember her first visit to Yellowstone. We worked here last summer just after she was born, but went back home for the winter. This year, we are staying on at the hotel as winter caretakers. My health isn't good, so I can't travel anymore."

I gazed at her in concern. Mattie was very pale and too thin. And her cough had sounded nasty. But her smile was sweet and she was good company on this warm autumn afternoon.

Mattie grinned suddenly at the little Clark's nutcracker, which had hopped closer as we talked, eyes still fixed on my trail mix. She hummed at the bird, who replied with a funny chittering sound. Suddenly the bird flew away, seemingly alarmed by something it heard. Mattie glanced toward the river, then rose and smiled at a man walking up the bank toward us. "There's my husband, Ellery. I must go. It was lovely speaking with you, Karen."

Mattie slipped from the bench and walked toward her husband.

"It was nice to meet you, Mattie," I said, watching the strolling man in bemused wonder. Mattie's husband was dressed in a conservative old suit that seemed to match Mattie's old-fashioned dress and coat. Ellery tipped his hat to me and offered Mattie his arm. They walked past me along the riverbank.

At that moment, a cold gust of wind whipped over the table, sending my napkin flying. I lunged for it and caught it before it fell off the table. When I turned back, the riverbank was empty. Mattie and Ellery had vanished as mysteriously as they'd arrived.

How odd, I thought and shivered in the sudden silence.

My fingers were trembling as I finished my lunch. I rubbed my goose-fleshed arms, feeling cold and a bit spooked. I glanced around, hoping to see the friendly Clark's nutcracker, but the bird, too, had vanished. I thrust the remainder of my meal into the picnic basket and got up quickly, no longer enjoying the view. It was time to move on.

As I turned toward the parking lot, I saw a small, fenced-in area behind the restrooms. The wooden posts resembled those I'd seen placed around thermal features that popped up unexpectedly in public parking lots. Speculating on what I might find—a mud pot? a fumarole?—I walked over to the fenced-off place, jauntily swinging my picnic basket.

What emerged as I walked down the sagebrush slope was a small, white grave with a rose carved on the front. I moved around the fence until I could read the writing on the tomb: MATTIE S. WIFE OF E. C. CULVER. DIED MARCH 2, 1889, AGED 30 YEARS.

I gasped and dropped the picnic basket, chills encompassing my body. I leaned heavily against the fence, legs trembling so fiercely that they would not hold me upright.

"Mattie!" I gasped. "Mattie!"

I had just had lunch with a ghost.

I drew in several ragged breaths, my heart pounding so hard it hurt my chest. Then I grabbed my picnic basket and ran for the car. I didn't care how nice Mattie was. I was getting out of here!

By the time I'd reached my little camper at Madison Junction, my heartbeat had slowed and I'd grown curious about my supernatural encounter. Over the next several days, I made cautious inquiries about Mattie's grave and learned more about her.

Martha Jane Gilbert was a widow living in a hotel in Billings, Montana, when she met Ellery Culver, the new hotel manager.

Mattie was struggling to make a new life for herself after her husband's death from tuberculosis. She and Ellery grew close and married in April 1886. Their daughter, Theda, was born a year later, and the young parents moved to Yellowstone, where Ellery had secured a job as the master of transportation. The Culver family spent the summer at the Firehole Hotel, which stood on the grounds that now houses the Nez Perce Picnic Area, and then the couple wintered in Billings. When they returned the next summer, it was clear that Mattie was dying of tuberculosis. She could not travel far in her invalid condition, so the Culvers overwintered in Yellowstone as caretakers of the hotel. Mattie passed away on March 2, 1889, just shy of her third wedding anniversary. She was buried in a grave a stone's throw from the Firehole Hotel, where she had lived and worked until her death.

After Mattie's death, little Theda went to live with her aunt, but Ellery returned to Yellowstone for many years to be near his beloved wife. The Firehole Hotel burned to the ground in 1891 and was not replaced. Ellery died in 1922 and was buried in California, where he'd spent his retirement years in an old soldier's home.

Over the years, many park visitors reported seeing Ellery's spirit walking the banks of the Firehole River in the company of his beloved wife, Mattie. And now I was among them.

Rest in peace, Ellery and Mattie Culver.

2

I Want to Go Home

I gasped a bit as I wheeled my heavy bag toward the white-trimmed double doors leading to the hotel lobby. I was having some trouble adjusting to the altitude in Yellowstone after living my whole life at sea level. I doddered my way into the lobby and staggered up to the front desk to check in.

Key in hand, I aimed myself somewhat erratically for the hall leading to the elevator. About halfway down, a compassionate bellman overtook me and claimed my heavy bag. Relieved, I hitched my handbag over my shoulder and followed the bellman. We chattered about my trip, and the bellman had some great suggestions for places along the lakeshore where I might see wildlife.

The elevator let us off on the fourth floor, and we walked to the end of a long, rather spooky hallway. I shivered a bit, feeling uncomfortable but not understanding why. The friendly bellman left me in front of the open door with my suitcase, bowing slightly like an old-fashioned gentleman in a movie. I fumbled in my handbag, looking for my wallet, but I couldn't find it. When I looked up from my bag, the bellman was gone. That was . . . strange. My neck prickled suddenly and I swallowed

I WANT TO GO HOME

hard. Supernatural things happened rather often to the members of my family, including me. The sudden disappearance of the bellman made me wonder if I had inadvertently booked a room in a haunted hotel.

I entered the room, which was quite lovely. It was at the end of the hall on the back side of the hotel, but I could see the lake out the side window. Still, something about the room felt a little strange, as if someone was watching me. I had goose bumps all along my upper arms as I hurriedly unpacked. I had reservations for 7:00 p.m. at the hotel dining room, and it was almost that time now.

The being-watched feeling returned in full force as I walked down the spooky hallway to the elevator. I shivered and wondered if I should go back to the room for my sweater. Then I remembered the disappearing bellman and opted to go on instead.

Dinner was lovely and quite restored my spirits. I had scheduled an early-morning photo tour, so I went to bed early, although I didn't sleep well. I was still uncomfortable with the spooky atmosphere of the room, and I kept jerking awake, expecting to see who knows what.

After a splendid day of taking pictures and touring West Thumb, I was hurrying downstairs for an early dinner reservation when I passed a group taking a tour of the hotel. At that moment, the tour guide was telling the story of a phantom bellman rumored to haunt the hotel. I stopped abruptly to listen. According to the story, the bellman sometimes helped people carry their luggage upstairs, and he always disappeared before the person could tip him. Happy customers usually stopped at the bell desk to compliment the hotel on such superior service. When asked to identify the staff member who had assisted them, the vacationers would inevitably point to a man that appeared in an historic photograph of the hotel bell staff that stood on the desk. The man in the photograph was a former bell captain who worked at the hotel in the early 1900s!

I took a deep breath and hurried down the hall. So now I knew who had helped me with my luggage. The thought gave me goose bumps.

After dinner, I spent the evening sitting in the lobby, gazing out at the lake and listening to a woman play the piano. The lobby itself was supposedly haunted by the ghost of a former president, but no supernatural presence disturbed my happy musings, for which I was grateful.

It was 3:00 a.m. when I jerked awake to find a dark shadow hovering over my head and torso. "I want to go home," I heard a voice say in my head. Then the shadow whooshed away, sending my hair flying away from my sleepy face. The wind of its passing rattled the lampshade beside the bed. I pulled the covers up to my chin, my body trembling from head to toe in fright. The room was perfectly still and growing colder by the second.

Then I heard a knocking sound from the wall by my bed. *Knock-knock. Knock-knock.* The hovering spirit wanted to come back into the room to talk to me, now that I was awake. In my experience, these late-night supernatural conversations didn't always go well.

"It is the middle of the night," I said sternly into the cold night air. "I need to rest. I will talk to you in the morning."

There was a sense of hesitation from the spirit in the hallway. Then I felt it accept my words and move away. I turned on my side and closed my eyes, determined to get some sleep. I would deal with the spirit in the morning.

I was walking down to breakfast the next morning when I heard a knocking sound from the wall beside the elevator. *Knock-knock*. It sounded like someone asking to come in. I had told the spirit I would talk to it in the morning. And it *was* morning.

I took a seat in one of the chairs in the little sitting area looking out over the lake. I drew in a deep breath and mentally invited the spirit to come in. Immediately, a shimmering column of air appeared beside me. "I want to go home," a voice said. It sounded like a child.

"Who are you?" I asked.

"Cheryl," said the column of light. "I want to go home."

"Wh—where is your home?" I asked.

The shimmering figure did not answer. Instead, it wailed, "Lost! Lonely!"

"I don't think you can go home, honey," I said gently. Not if she was dead. "Shouldn't you be in heaven?"

I sensed puzzlement from the shimmering figure. "You have to go to the light, Cheryl," I told her.

Apparently, it was the right thing to say. I felt dawning comprehension from the shimmering column of air. Then it vanished. Immediately, the temperature in the sitting area rose by about ten degrees. I took in a gasping breath, realizing that I was trembling with nerves.

I rose on shaking legs and headed back to my room for my luggage, deciding I wanted to skip breakfast. Between disappearing bellmen and shimmering columns of air, I was pretty spooked by this hotel. It was time to check out.

"I just hope that Old Faithful Inn isn't haunted, too," I muttered to myself as I trundled my bag out to the car.

3

The Ghost in the Green Shirt

JACKSON LAKE

When John Sargent first came to visit Jackson Hole 'round about 1886, I didn't know what to make of him. Sargent was tall and slim with fine features, straight black hair, and a black mustache. He talked like some posh Eastern city slicker, but he claimed to have worked as a cowpoke down Colorado way—and the way he had with horses pretty much proved him right. About that time, Jackson Hole was full of trappers, gunslingers, rogues, and women of dubious character. None of them warmed up to Sargent, who talked about art and music and city slicker stuff.

Sargent kept popping up now and again in Jackson Hole and eventually bought land up on Jackson Lake. The spot he chose was one of the prettiest in the whole West. It had a jaw-dropping view of the jagged Grand Teton Mountains, which reflected grandly on the water when the wind was still.

Sargent and his family moved to the lake in 1890 and started building their spread. The new homestead was just off the road to Yellowstone National Park, and Sargent figured he'd make a mint providing overnight lodging for tourists heading up to see Old Faithful.

'Round about the same time, another city slicker named Robert Hamilton came to Jackson Hole, trailing scandal and broken heart. The fellow'd been taken to the cleaners by a gal back east, and he was eager to make a new start. Sargent and Hamilton hit it off as soon as they met. Hamilton loved the Grand Tetons, and he was excited by the possibilities of Sargent's homestead on the lake. A partnership was proposed and accepted, money changed hands, and construction commenced on the fancy ten-room Sargent-Hamilton cabin.

Then tragedy struck. On August 23, 1890, Robert Hamilton went out alone to hunt antelope, which were plentiful in the region. On his way back to the cabin, Hamilton attempted to ford the Snake River in the dark, fell from his horse, and drowned in the river when his spurs tangled with the weeds on the bottom.

Sargent was in Idaho at the time, getting supplies and mail. When he returned to the lake on August 27, he organized a search party to look for Robert, who was several days overdue. Hamilton's drowned body was found on September 2.

Sargent was now in sole possession of the lucrative new ranch, a circumstance that folks in town found mighty suspicious. There was talk of foul play, but no one could prove it. Me, I thought folks were just being spiteful.

When the Sargent ranch—now called Marymere—was completed in 1891, it was pretty posh, with a barn, a stable, a chicken house, a woodshed, and spacious corrals. Inside the ten-room cabin, Sargent kept a big library, a pool table, and one of those fancy phonographs. My favorite building was the fancy boathouse he had brought over from Idaho. Sargent had a boat in there that could be both rowed and sailed, since it was outfitted with a mast.

THE GHOST IN THE GREEN SHIRT

In early September, when the aspens were golden and the air was chilly and sweet, Sargent took me sailing on the lake. I was his closest neighbor at the time and had done a spot of work for him, helping with his stock and whatnot. The boat ride was his way of thanking me for a job well done. As the wind filled the sail and the waves lapped the sides of the boat, Sargent said wistfully, "Robert was really excited when I suggested getting a boat. He loved the water and often spoke of rowing himself all over the lake."

It was the first time I'd heard Sargent speak of his dead partner. I nodded in sympathy and glanced over at the rugged city slicker. His dark eyes were far away. He pointed suddenly toward the bay.

"There," he said. "That's where I saw him."

"Saw who?" I asked, confused by the change in topic.

"Robert," Sargent replied. "It was about midnight on August 23, and I couldn't sleep. Too many thoughts rolling inside my head. So I went down to sit by the water, hoping the lap of the waves would soothe me. Suddenly, there was Robert, clear as day, wearing his green shirt and rowing a glowing boat across the bay."

Goose bumps raced along my arms and legs. I glanced nervously at Sargent, recalling that August 23 was the day Robert Hamilton had drowned in the Snake River.

Suddenly, I wanted out of that boat. I was half a mile from shore in the company of a man accused of murdering his partner. This self-same man had just confessed that he'd seen his partner's ghost on the anniversary of the drowning. A coincidence? Maybe not. I wondered how long it would take me to swim to shore if I jumped out of the boat right here and now.

But Sargent had already moved on. When I roused from my internal speculations, he was discussing the music of someone named Beethoven. I figured I was safe for the moment. But I was never so happy to set foot on dry land.

Sargent mentioned the ghost a couple more times over the years. He saw the glowing figure rowing across the bay every year at midnight on August the twenty-third. I got the impression that he stayed up specially to watch for it. I could tell the ghost sightings troubled the city-slicker-turned-rancher. His hands shook whenever he spoke about it, and his body sweated profusely, as if he'd been running for miles. The smell of sour armpits was not pleasant, let me tell you, and the crazed look in Sargent's eyes when he spoke of the ghost was even worse.

Sargent and his missus operated the Marymere Ranch as a dude and hunting ranch for several years. Then tragedy struck once again. On a frigid day in March 1897, a group of Jackson Hole residents forcibly removed a very ill Mrs. Sargent from the Marymere Ranch and transported her by toboggan to the D. C. Nowlin ranch some fifty miles south. Mrs. Sargent's condition worsened despite all nursing efforts, and she died on April 11, 1897.

The whole community was in an uproar over Adelaide Sargent's death. This was the second suspicious death associated with the disliked Sargent, and many sensational and contradictory accounts appeared in the newspapers. Some folks claimed that Sargent had beaten his wife and she had died of her wounds. Others said he'd starved her and refused to send for the doctor when she fell ill. Sargent himself reported that his wife was with child and that she'd died from complications of her pregnancy. In the end, Sargent was arrested and accused of murdering his wife. But the case was dismissed due to conflicting statements from eyewitnesses and lack of evidence.

Folks in Jackson Hole were furious when Sargent was set free. The gossips and busybodies discussed drowned Robert and half-starved Adelaide until I wanted to throw my boots at them. Sargent had a hunted look about him when he returned to Jackson Lake, like he was afraid the devil would get him. He was deeply depressed and lived a reclusive life on his ranch. I couldn't blame him. Sargent was a sensitive, literate man, with a fine library collection and many phonograph recordings that demonstrated his appreciation for the fine arts and humanities. Such a man, if he was innocent of wrongdoing, would feel the slander against him keenly.

The story of the ghost in the green shirt that rowed across the bay on the anniversary of Robert's death grew very popular around this time. Why else would such a ghost appear, unless the drowned man in question was really murdered? So said the busybodies, and most everyone believed them.

Sargent married again in 1906. His new wife was another eastern lady who didn't fit in with Jackson Hole society. Rumor said the new wife was mentally ill and that Sargent was being paid by her family to take care of her. In 1912, the new Mrs. Sargent went to live with her sister in California, claiming that she wanted to start a new life and a new business. She hoped to entice her depressed husband to join her there, but Sargent was too strongly attached to his homestead and Jackson Hole to leave the land he loved.

In June 1913, John Sargent placed the barrel of his 40-90 rifle in his mouth, tied one end of a string to the trigger and the other to his big toe, and shot himself while the phonograph played "Ye Who Have Yearned Alone" in the background. The lead from the shell was found in the wall above the door of his living room.

At midnight on August 23 of the same year, I sat on the bank of Jackson Lake in the place so frequently occupied by my neighbor and watched as a ghost in a green shirt rowed a glowing boat across the bay. It seemed a fitting farewell to my much-maligned neighbor.

4

The Headless Bride

OLD FAITHFUL

The campfire blazed up in the grate, its heat gradually warming the frosty night air around us. Our daughters were roasting marshmallows over the flames, and my wife, Tina, held chocolate and graham crackers on her lap, ready to make s'mores when they were finished.

"Tell us a story, Daddy," my eldest daughter requested. Jeri was a blue-eyed cherub with white-blond hair and an angelic smile. Her appearance was utterly misleading. Whenever there was mischief in our household, Jeri was at the bottom of it. (She was a lot like her dad.)

I knew this particular request was a ploy to put off bedtime. Jeri hated going to sleep and always did her best to put it off. Still, it was a holiday weekend. We could let them stay up for once.

"A ghost story," chimed in Theresa, who was dark-haired and gray-eyed, like her beautiful mom. Theresa had also inherited her mother's angelic personality, although it was admittedly tarnished by association with her mischievous sister.

I was crazy about my girls, but not above teasing them from time to time. (All the time, my wife claimed.)

21

"I don't know any stories," I said, leaning back on my log and accepting a s'more from my younger daughter's hand.

"You do, too!" shrieked Jeri, pouncing onto my lap with a charcoaled marshmallow on the end of her stick. I found myself staring cross-eyed at the marshmallow waving in front of my nose as she continued, "I heard you ask the ranger about ghosts while we were watching Old Faithful erupt this afternoon."

"Watch where you put that stick, Jeri! You'll poke Daddy's eye out," Tina scolded, rising in wrath from her seat by the fire to take marshmallow and stick from her eldest.

"What did the ranger say, Daddy?" asked Theresa, sitting down next to me on the log. She took a thoughtful bite of her s'more, sending crumbs of graham cracker sprinkling down on her lap.

"There are a couple of old legends about the inn," I said, putting my arm around Theresa and giving Jeri a squeeze while I was at it. "Some people say that the ghost of a lost boy haunts the second story of the Old Faithful Inn. He's always looking for someone to help him find his parents. And then there is the tale of the headless bride. That's just a made-up story, but it's pretty spooky. You wouldn't want to hear it just before bed," I teased.

"Tell us! Tell us!" The girls bounced up and down in their excitement. Jeri almost knocked me off the log. I removed her from my lap and put her beside her sister.

"If I do, you must promise to go to sleep tonight. No nightmares," I said sternly.

"We promise," the girls said together.

"Anyway, I'm not scared of ghosts," said Jeri airily.

Not yet, I thought wickedly, and began my tale.

"Once there was a lovely young woman growing up in a wealthy shipping family in New York. In those days, rich young women were expected to make their debut in society and to marry a rich young man from a good family. But our young lady was a bit of a rebel. When she grew old enough to marry, she scorned the wealthy young society men in favor of a handsome servant who worked in her house," I told the girls, watching the firelight flickering in their eager eyes.

"Of course, there was a big argument when the young woman announced her choice of husband," I continued. "Her parents were furious, particularly her father, who accused the servant of courting his wealthy daughter and to gain a prominent position in the shipping company. When the young lady insisted upon the marriage, her father gave the couple a lump sum of cash with the stipulation that the couple leave New York after the wedding and never come back."

"That's mean," Theresa broke in.

"It's the way things were back then," I said. "Do you want me to continue?"

The girls nodded vigorously, and Jeri poked her sister with her elbow, whispering, "Hush, or he'll make us go to bed!"

I smiled and related the following details in the flickering light of our fall campfire:

By the time the young couple reached the Old Faithful Inn in Yellowstone, the new husband had gambled away all of the money that his wife's family had bestowed upon the newlyweds. There was barely enough money for the couple to finish their honeymoon trip, and nothing whatsoever with which to buy a house or start a family.

The young woman was upset with her new husband. They quarreled often about money, and she finally understood that her father had been right about the man. He was only interested in her money. The first night at the inn, the new husband lost the last of their funds in a poker game, and the woman was forced to telephone her father to ask him for a loan. Her father told her she was in a mess of her own making and refused to give her any more money.

That night, the couple had a terrific fight in the privacy of their bedroom at the inn. The husband stalked out of the inn in a fury, leaving his bride locked in her room with a Do Not Disturb sign hanging on the door. The bride did not emerge for several days.

Finally, the staff of the inn sent someone to check on her. No one answered when the housekeeper knocked on the door. Using the master key, the housekeeper stepped into the room and gasped in shock. The room looked as if a hurricane had swept through it. Clothes were strewn everywhere, and the bedclothes were partially on the floor. Worse, the housekeeper was overwhelmed by a musky metallic odor that permeated everything. There was no sign of the bride, but the stink that wafted from the attached bathroom hinted at what the housekeeper might see. Lying in the bathtub in a pool of congealed blood lay the headless body of the unhappy bride, blood spattered all over her dress and clumped grotesquely on the ragged remains of her neck. Her head was nowhere to be seen.

The housekeeper's screams alerted the rest of the staff. The authorities were summoned, the family was notified, and the room was examined for evidence and then cleaned. Everything was done to locate the husband who had murdered her, but

THE HEADLESS BRIDE

he was never found. Finally, the whole story was hushed up to avoid scandal to the prominent eastern family who'd lost their only daughter.

About a week after the murder, a foul smell up in the Crows Nest, where the musicians played for the evening dances, was traced to its source: the bride's severed head. Tousled blond curls framed a wide-eyed, horror-twisted face already beginning to rot.

The burial of the poor, murdered bride should have been the end of the terrible incident. And so it proved to be, until one midnight when a staff member up late reading a book heard a strange noise coming from the lobby. At the stroke of midnight, he hurried onto the balcony and looked upward, seeking the source of the noise. In the Crows Nest far above, he saw a glowing figure in white walk to the top of the stairs and slowly descend. Tucked under its arm was a tousle-curled, horror-twisted head! Frozen with terror, the man watched the headless bride descend the steps and float along the corridor until she reached the door of the room where she was murdered. Then she vanished!

Both girls jumped in alarm when I said "vanished." Theresa gave a little wail and vanished too, flinging herself through the open door of our RV. We heard footsteps pound along the length of the camper and a huge thump as she threw herself into the back bed. Tina and I stared at each other in alarm. But before we could move, Theresa reappeared in the door of the RV, clutching her favorite pillow in front of her like a shield. "Go on, Daddy," she said from the safety of the doorway. "What happened next?"

Relieved, I went on. "From that day onward, there have been people who say they can see the headless bride walking down the stairs from the Crows Nest at the stroke of midnight, sadly seeking her lost husband and her lost dreams. Myself, I've never stayed up to see."

There was a long silence, broken only by the crackle of the flames and the thud of a falling log. Finally, Jeri shook her shoulders and rose from the log. "Great story, Dad," she said, her voice quavering slightly. "Come on, Theresa. Time for bed."

Time for bed? Words I had never before heard my precocious daughter utter. Jeri always gave us grief at bedtime. The girls disappeared into the RV, leaving Tina and I staring at one another, completely flummoxed. We waited five minutes to give them time to settle. Then we tiptoed into the RV. We found the girls buried under the covers with their pillows over their heads! They were fast asleep.

"Well," Tina whispered softly. "After all these years, we've finally discovered the perfect solution to bedtime. Ghost stories! Who knew?"

We chuckled softly and went back outside to sit by the flickering fire, drink hot cocoa, and look at the stars.

5

Hello Darlin'

CODY

The scientists called it clairaudience. I had to look up the definition of the word when I was first diagnosed with this rare paranormal ability. Apparently, clairaudient people like me have psi-mediated hearing. We hear things that other people can't—like the voices of ghosts and secrets whispered on the wind. Clairaudients don't always hear sounds out loud. Sometimes we get impressions in our inner mental ear, similar to the way many people can think words without speaking out loud. But we also hear real sounds—voices, tones, or noises—that are not apparent to other humans or to recording equipment.

When I was a child, it never bothered me that I could hear invisible people talking. I thought everyone could. It was only when I became a teenager and the voices started telling me things I could not possibly know that I became worried. My grandmother's will was missing when she died, but I knew right away where to find it because she came and told me. She sat invisibly on the end of my bed and said, "Sarah, it is under a floorboard in the attic. The one that has a knothole shaped like a cat." And sure enough, there it was.

HELLO DARLIN'

About a week after my neighbor's dog went missing, an invisible dog bumped into my legs as I was getting off the school bus. Its bark sounded just like my neighbor's dog, and as it licked my hands I smelt almonds on its breath. A heartbeat later, I heard a man's voice calling its name. I knew that voice. It belonged to Old Henry, who lived on the street behind my neighbor's house. At that moment, I realized that Old Henry, who complained frequently about the barking, had poisoned my neighbor's dog. I mentioned the incident to my parents, who told the police, who found the dog's body buried under Old Henry's woodpile.

After the incident with the dog, my parents were pretty freaked. They found a lab where I could have my paranormal abilities tested scientifically. The scientists were very excited by my ability to sense and hear things that I should never have been able to sense and hear. In the end, my parents called a halt to the testing. They wanted me to grow up as a normal girl and not as a science experiment. So I went back to school and lived a normal teenage life. I just had a few extra senses that I didn't talk about, except when I was alone with my parents. But I studied all I could about other people who had clairaudient abilities, which helped me feel normal.

By the time I graduated from college and found a job, being clairaudient was just a normal part of life. I always knew which houses and buildings were haunted, even if there was no official record of the haunting. I could sense the presence of the ghosts even if I couldn't see them. And sometimes those ghosts spoke to me. I think they were glad to talk to someone who could hear them so clearly. Many of them were lonely.

However, I wasn't thinking about ghosts when I stopped overnight at Cody, on my way to Yellowstone National Park.

My mind was full of bison herds and geysers and hot springs. I might even get to see one of the elusive wolves that lived in Lamar Valley!

But that was tomorrow. Today, I was in Cody, and I had arrived in town early enough to take in some of the sights for which Cody was justly famous. So I tossed my suitcase on the hotel bed and hurried to catch the trolley tour, which left from the front of the Buffalo Bill Museum. It was well worth the admission fee. The tour guides were a hoot. Well-scripted patter, fun facts, great old photos blown up to poster size so they were easy to see. I loved it.

After the tour, I explored the local Buffalo Bill Museum, viewing the art gallery and learning everything I could about William Cody—American soldier, bison hunter, and world-famous showman.

Buffalo Bill rode with the Pony Express, then worked for the US Army as a scout. But what he was most famous for was Buffalo Bill's Wild West, a cowboy-themed, circus-like show that romanticized the Old West. The show toured all over the United States and gave performances in Great Britain and Europe. Cody had headliners such as sharpshooter Annie Oakley and her husband Frank Butler. Other performers reenacted the riding of the Pony Express, Indian attacks on wagon trains, and stagecoach robberies. The finale of Buffalo Bill's Wild West was typically a portrayal of an Indian attack on a settler's cabin. Cody would ride heroically in with an entourage of cowboys to defend the settler and his family.

Buffalo Bill was instrumental in the founding of Cody, Wyoming. When Cody first passed through the region, he was so impressed by the development possibilities due to rich soil, grand scenery, hunting, and proximity to Yellowstone Park that he returned in 1895 to start a town. In 1902, Cody opened the Irma Hotel, which he named after his daughter. To accommodate Yellowstone travelers, Cody completed construction of the Wapiti Inn and Pahaska Tepee by the East Entrance in 1905.

Cody died of kidney failure on January 10, 1917, surrounded by family and friends at his sister's house in Denver, Colorado. He was buried, against the wishes stated in his will, on Lookout Mountain in Golden, Colorado.

My head swimming with facts about Buffalo Bill Cody, I returned to my hotel room to relax with a book before heading out to the Irma to watch a staged gunfight in the street beside the hotel. Lots of "big names" showed up as characters in the show: Buffalo Bill, Wyatt Earp, Kit Carson, Doc Holliday. My ears started ringing from all the gunfire, but all in all it was a great performance and some of the jokes had me in stitches.

I'd planned to eat in the historic dining room of the Irma Hotel, but apparently so had nearly everyone else at the gunfight! I entered the front hallway in a swarm of people and halted so fast that a man bumped into me from behind. This hotel was haunted. I knew it immediately. As the crowd streamed around me, I stretched out my sixth sense, wondering if I should turn around and have dinner at the Italian place down the street.

I hesitated for a moment, but I wasn't sensing any hostility from the presences I felt at the hotel—three of them. One was on the top floor. One was in the restaurant. The other roamed the whole hotel.

None of the ghosts made any attempt to contact me, so I decided it was safe to eat dinner at the Irma. I ended up at a table in the lounge since the restaurant was so crowded. I ordered the chicken potpie (yum) preceded by the salad bar.

As I made my way into the restaurant to visit the salad bar, I passed a booth in the back that was occupied by a noisy family and the silent ghost of a man. Businessman? Cowboy? I wasn't sure. He didn't speak to me and I didn't ask. I just dumped salad, dressing, and croutons on my plate and hurried back to the noise and bustle of the lounge.

About three-quarters of the way through my meal, the seat beside me quavered as if someone had just sat down in it. I blinked and stared at the blank space. I had the oddest sensation that Buffalo Bill himself had just joined me for dinner.

"Hello darlin'," a man drawled from the empty seat beside me. It was definitely Bill Cody.

"Greetings," I said quietly. I diligently applied myself to the rest of my dinner, aware that I was being watched. A few moments later the server brought me my check, and I gathered up my bags to leave.

"Don't go so soon," my invisible companion begged. He followed me into a long hallway filled with life-size animal heads and a large carving of an Indian standing beside the door to the gift shop. I hesitated, caught by the pleading note in his voice.

"Well," I said silently, "I *haven't* photographed your 'original cherry wood bar.'" I gestured to the sign advertising the historic antique that graced the wall beside the restaurant door.

"Then by all means, let's have a look," the ghost of Buffalo Bill Cody said with a bow. He swept past me into the restaurant, and I followed my spirited host into the main dining room.

I took out my camera and took photos of the long cherry wood bar from various angles, aware that the temperature beside the bar was several degrees lower than anywhere else in the room. I walked through three different cold spots as I moved from one end of the bar to the other. The air swirled around me strangely, even though no fans or air-conditioner vents were nearby. (I checked.)

"What do you think, darlin'?" my host asked when I was done with my photographs.

"Very nice," I told him.

"Glad you like it, darlin'," said the spirit of Bill Cody in a flirtatious manner.

"Don't you be flirting with me," I said severely. "You are a married man!"

"Oh, Lou!" The ghost of Buffalo Bill sighed his wife's name with a mixture of frustration and pride. I grinned in sympathy. According to the information in the museum, Bill and his wife had had a rocky marriage. They'd been in divorce court at least once. It occurred to me that Bill Cody was dead now, so technically they were no longer married. I decided not to bring it up.

"I must go," I said, feeling uncomfortable standing around the restaurant with my camera without ordering anything. The place was bustling with people, and I was in the way here.

"Don't go yet," said the ghost of Bill Cody. But I knew it was time to leave.

"You can walk me to the door," I said. We walked beside the door to the front of the restaurant. Wherever we passed, people shivered and pulled on their jackets, or straightened hair that the mysterious, swirling breeze had mussed.

The ghost of Buffalo Bill Cody waved me goodbye from the front stoop. Just for an instant, I saw a flash of white that might have been a man in a cowboy hat and fringed jacket. I wished my paranormal abilities included the ability to see ghosts.

"Good-bye," I called. "May all go well for you."

And then I was alone.

6

Fatal Feud

BIG SKY

He was a surly old prospector who came to Cooke City in 1897 looking for gold. He'd had his fill of working on ranches and wanted to strike it rich. Armed with a pickax and a shovel, he wandered the steep mountains and valleys, examining every stream and river for glints of gold. He slept each night under the stars except when it rained. Then he curled up under a pine.

When he found a promising spot, he threw up a shack for himself near a stream and set some traps, intending to supplement his prospecting by selling furs. He spent the days panning, and in the evenings he checked traps and cooked supper on an open fire. After eating his vittles, he'd sit on a fallen log and watch the sun set over the mountain peaks while his dog Shep hunted chipmunks in the sagebrush.

A hermit by nature, he kept his interactions with fellow humans brief and to the point. He had no time for nonsense, especially not from the female half of the species. Still, he couldn't help running into folks when he went to the settlement for supplies, and that's how he met Mrs. Miller, the most aggravating female in the whole darn West.

The old man wasn't a particularly good prospector. After a decade of solitude and scraping by on what he could trade for gold dust and furs, the prospector threw in the towel. Time to try something else.

Unfortunately, the only job to hand was working on the Miller ranch for that horrible she-cat, now a widow of several years. Being a cowboy and general ranch hand didn't suit him after spending so much time as a prospector. And Mrs. Miller drove him plumb crazy with her nagging about every little thing. So the old prospector squirreled away every penny for five long years, until he had enough money to file a claim on some land just northeast of the Miller place. After saying farewell to the troublesome Mrs. Miller, the old prospector settled down with Shep and a couple of cats.

The old prospector was thrilled to his boots at the freedom of owning his own spread. He put in a big garden and ran a few head of cattle. He had enough money left over from the purchase to invest in a barn and a few horses. He even started prospecting again, hoping to find some gold or sapphires on his land. His luck had turned at last.

Then Mrs. Miller started calling on him at his new spread; unannounced, unwelcome, and quarrelsome as ever. One day she turned out his horses and berated him for leaving his job. Another day she struck his team with a whip, causing them to bolt with his wagon. She once pulled a gun on him when he was down in the root cellar. When he refused to hitch up her team, Mrs. Miller threatened to poison him. She let her cows graze on his pastureland, and when he went to her ranch to discuss the matter, he found the widow "entertaining" some chap she'd met in town. The chap left in a hurry while the old prospector traded insults with the disheveled woman.

The old prospector asked the sheriff in to mediate between them, hoping that would solve the fierce feuding, but it had the opposite effect. Inflamed with rage, Mrs. Miller snuck onto his property while he was in town, stole thirty cabbages, and poisoned his provisions. The old prospector took one bite of the tainted food and realized that something wasn't right. He gave the meal to his cat, and it died a few hours later.

The old prospector reported the harassment to the local police, who took samples of the poisoned food and looked at the woman's footprints around his cabin, but nothing was done to curb the quarrelsome Mrs. Miller.

Just after the first snowfall, Mrs. Miller paid a man to shoot the old prospector. He took a bullet in the chest and spent many days recovering in the hospital in Butte. While he was in the hospital, his cabin was looted.

Mrs. Miller continued to harass the old prospector through the long winter and the spring that followed. On a warm day in June, the old prospector returned home to find his front door open and the water bucket full of poison. It was the last straw. Grabbing his rifle, he went to confront Mrs. Miller with her crimes. After searching all the obvious places, he swung around for a second look through his fields. From the top of a ridge, he saw Mrs. Miller picking her way daintily along a shortcut that ran through his alfalfa bed. When the old prospector shouted, "Stop," the irksome Mrs. Miller drew her revolver. It was the same weapon the hired killer had used to shoot him in the chest. Panicked, the old prospector raised his rifle and shot his would-be assassin. Mrs. Miller let out a faint cry and collapsed face down in the alfalfa.

Dazed, the old prospector stared at her dead body for what seemed hours. Then fear took over. What if someone saw him

FATAL FEUD

here with the corpse of the widow? He went back to his cabin and sat for hours trying to decide what to do. The woman had stolen from him, poisoned him, shot him. But he hadn't meant to kill her. Should he turn himself in? He thought of all the times he'd gone to the sheriff and the sheriff had done nothing to help him. If they wouldn't help when Mrs. Miller poisoned him and had him shot, would they take pity on him now? Not likely.

After dark, the old prospector returned to the alfalfa field. In the darkness, he knelt by the body and moaned, "Oh, girl, if you'd left me alone, this would never have happened." Picking up the stiffened body, he lugged it into the hills. He spent the rest of the night digging a grave using tools fetched from his cabin. It was dawn when he collapsed on his bed, too exhausted to move for the rest of the day.

Around eleven o'clock that night, the old prospector was jerked out of his uneasy doze by rapping and wailing sounds from the roof. The stovepipe rattled as the sounds grew louder. The old prospector clapped his hands over his ears as the wailing rose higher and higher. Then he heard Mrs. Miller's sobbing voice. "Help! Help!" she screamed and then gasped. It was the noise she'd made when his bullet hit her. The small gasp chilled the old prospector worse than the wailing. "Miz Miller! I'm sorry, I'm sorry," he cried, rearing up in his bed with tears streaming down his face.

The sound changed to a low groan. Mrs. Miller's voice rang out again: "Sheriff! Arrest him! He did it." The groaning began again, deeper this time with high overtones that raised every hair on the old prospector's body. He raced outside the cabin. "What do you want?" he shouted at the empty roof. But he knew. Oh yes, *he knew.*

The nights that followed were an agony for the old prospector. During the day, he could forget his crime . . . mostly. He put two stumps over the fresh grave to camouflage it. Then he went about his daily chores as if nothing had happened. But at night. . . . Sometimes he'd sleep for several hours before the rapping and moaning began. Sometimes it would start as soon as he lay down. Some nights, he would hear Mrs. Miller's voice accusing him of various crimes, just as she'd done in life. Some nights, she would scream for the sheriff.

The old prospector decided to sell his claim before he went insane. But the spirit of Mrs. Miller sensed his decision and began haunting him during the day. She rapped on fence posts and moaned on the wind. Her voice berated him in the barn, out in the fields, and up by the dam.

The day he glimpsed her face in the window of the local mercantile, he knew Mrs. Miller's accusing spirit would follow him wherever he went. He'd have to turn himself in or go mad. And so he took his story to the sheriff and led a posse to the hidden body.

As the old prospector had feared, the jury refused to believe his plea of self-defense, and he was sentenced to life imprisonment. When the prison doors closed on him for the last time, he thought he heard the ghost of Mrs. Miller laugh.

7

Ghost Train

GARDINER

My buddy Cooper and I sat in the bar nursing our drinks while we waited for our dinner reservations. Cooper was trying—and failing—to stay awake after our strenuous hike up Mount Washburn in Yellowstone National Park.

"So what should we do tomorrow?" I asked lazily, eyeing the pretty server who flitted past on her way to a table. "We haven't hiked the Canyon area yet."

"No hiking," groaned Cooper into his beer mug, making little waves splash against the sides. "I propose we sit in front of the TV and veg."

"You'll stiffen up," I said. "If you're going to sit all day, I suggest you sit in the pools down by the Boiling River."

Cooper perked up at the mention of the Boiling River, Yellowstone National Park's most popular soaking area. It was easily accessible from the North Entrance Road, and the gorgeous mountain location couldn't be beat. Geologists speculated that the Boiling River's one-hundred-yard channel of 140-degree water was the underground flow from Mammoth Hot Springs, some two miles to the south. The Boiling River emptied into a fifty-yard-long band of thermal soaking pools

GHOST TRAIN

along the Gardner River and was a wonderful spot to soak away the pain in overworked muscles.

"I think we should take a short hike tomorrow, just to stay limber," I said, gulping down the last of my beer and tossing money onto the bar. "Then we can take a long soak at the Boiling River pools. Maybe the folks at our hotel will have a hiking recommendation. Come on, it's almost time for dinner."

Cooper dragged himself off the bar stool, and we headed up the road to our restaurant.

Over dinner, our server recommended that we hike out to Cinnabar, the old ghost town that once held the terminus for the railroad line leading to Yellowstone. The little town was created abruptly by the railroad in 1883 after a land dispute with a local man kept them from continuing the track to Gardiner. In its heyday, Cinnabar acted as the "Western White House" for President Theodore Roosevelt and his entourage when the president came to Yellowstone to dedicate the grand arch at the North Entrance.

"Not much left out there," the server continued. "No buildings or anything. But you can still see the marks from the old track and some shallow foundation pits where the houses stood. It's not too far from the Devil's Slide."

The Devil's Slide was an unusual cliff rock formation on the side of Cinnabar Mountain. Standing at a height of 125 feet, the near-vertical rock slide was named by the Washburn Expedition that explored Yellowstone in 1871. At the time, it was thought that the exposed rock was made of cinnabar, a red mercury ore, though today's geologists said the slide contained iron oxide that was uplifted from an ancient marine seabed due to shifting plate tectonics.

Having observed the formation on the drive from Bozeman, I could understand exactly why it had been given its nickname. It looked as if the devil had decided to slide down the side of the hill on a toboggan, burning away all the vegetation and leaving a long red streak behind him.

"The whole Cinnabar region is part of Yellowstone now," the server continued. "It was included as part of the Gardiner Game Ranch addition back in 1932."

It sounded like a fairly easy hike, at least compared to yesterday, and it would give us something to look at besides sagebrush. We got directions and thanked her for the recommendation.

I asked for more information about Cinnabar when we got back to the hotel. Apparently, Cinnabar was the place where Yellowstone visitors were outfitted for their excursions and boarded stagecoaches for multiday tours. It was also where the troops stationed in the park disembarked from the train and were issued their horses. In addition to the railroad depot, the Cinnabar of that time had a hotel, a couple of saloons, a general store, a saw mill, and a rodeo ground that was used to hold auditions for riders and ropers for Buffalo Bill Cody's Wild West Show.

Near the railroad depot, a motley array of street vendors hawked Yellowstone souvenirs, including "Specimen Schmidt," who sold petrified wood, and Calamity Jane, who sometimes appeared in Buffalo Bill's Wild West Show as a horse rider and a trick shooter. Cinnabar was populated by an assorted crowd of hunters, trappers, traders, and grizzled old pioneers, to say nothing of gamblers, roughs, and desperadoes. Cinnabar sounded like the epitome of the Wild West to me. I was eager to view the site of the old ghost town, even if there wasn't much to see but sagebrush.

It was tough getting up the next morning after our strenuous mountain hike of the previous day. Cooper wouldn't budge before eight-thirty, and it was nearing ten when we hiked out to Old Stagecoach Road, which led to Cinnabar.

We were surrounded by the Rocky Mountains on all sides, but here in the river valley, most of the trail was open and exposed. The wind was so fierce that I almost lost my hat. It looked as if a storm was blowing in. We might get rained on during our ghost-town adventure, but neither Cooper nor I minded getting wet.

A grazing herd of pronghorn stopped to stare at Cooper and me from their chosen place among the prairie grass and sagebrush not far from the Yellowstone River. "Keep on eating," Cooper said. "We won't disturb you." The pronghorn seemed to take him at his word, for all but one returned to their meal as we continued our walk along the dirt-and-gravel road.

It was a bit hard to locate Cinnabar at first. There really was nothing left but some depressions that might have been the foundations of old buildings and a few scattered artifacts. I tried to imagine what Cinnabar must have looked like in its heyday: railroad depot, hotel, blacksmith shop. I pictured Calamity Jane selling souvenirs to gawking tourists and grand stagecoaches drawing up to escort passengers to the hotel in Mammoth. I searched around for the railroad tracks. I finally located a section of turf with ruts that seemed too straight to be natural.

A few yards away, Cooper stooped to examine the grass growing in a depression that might once have been a foundation.

"Don't disturb anything," I said sternly. "The server said an archeological dig will be conducted here next year."

"Wasn't planning to disturb anything," Cooper said mildly, sitting down on a rock and digging in his backpack. "You'd better put on your rain jacket," he continued. "Those storm clouds are rolling in fast."

The light was dimming rapidly as I hauled out my rain jacket and zipped it up. A cold storm wind blew across the mountains and whipped around us. The clouds were black as pitch and filled the sky from one end to the other, trapping us within this river valley. The pronghorns, I noticed, had fled the open fields to seek some sheltered spot. They were smarter than us. I saw a flash of lightning over a mountain peak as the storm twilight fell over the valley.

Suddenly, a brilliant light shone from the far side of the valley near the Devil's Slide.

"What's that?" asked Cooper with interest, coming to stand beside me.

"I have no idea," I said.

A train whistle blew suddenly in the distance, reverberating across the river valley. The light grew brighter, coming closer, and I saw a large black engine steaming its way out of Yankee Jim Canyon, heading our way almost as fast as the storm. It rattled and roared along invisible tracks, hissing every time it released steam. Combined with the howling wind, the sound was deafening.

Cooper observed the ghost train dispassionately. "I count five passenger cars," he said. "Plus the engine and the coal car. We may want to move," he added calmly as the ghost train came hurtling toward us.

"No kidding," I shouted, pushing him to one side of the phantom track as I flung myself into the sagebrush on the other side. The train roared past and then started slowing down as it drew near the phantom depot. I could almost make out the shimmering outline of the terminus building as the coal-black ghost train blew its whistle once, twice, and then shuddered to a halt. The smell of burning coal filled the air as droplets of steam mixed with the first drops of rain from the swirling thunder clouds.

Then the storm clouds opened up above us and the ghost train vanished, leaving us alone in the wide meadow between the Rocky Mountain peaks, with a wet journey back to our Gardiner hotel.

The wind was at our backs on the homeward journey. Cooper didn't say much as we sloshed through mud puddles and hunched deeply into our coats against the downpour. He pointed out a stone circle that might have been an old tipi ring or perhaps a prehistoric site of some kind. But that was his only comment until we reached our hotel.

"I don't remember our server mentioning a ghost train," Cooper said, throwing me a towel from the bathroom.

"Maybe it was a special performance, just for us," I said, catching the towel and rubbing my soaking hair vigorously. I'd turned on the heater in our room and was huddled over it, trying to stop trembling. I'd like to think the cold I was feeling came from the rainstorm, but I suspected that my shakes were due to the ghostly scene we'd observed in Cinnabar.

"It will make an interesting addition to my memoirs," Cooper said, disappearing into the bathroom. "Not that anyone will believe me," he added as he closed the door.

The rain stopped while we ate lunch, so we donned our swim trunks and headed over to the Boiling River for the afternoon. Cooper sighed with relief as he settled into a nicely warmed section of the middle soak pool. Behind him, a six-foot-wide hot stream of water poured over a travertine ledge, while cool water from the swift-flowing Gardner River eddied around him, chilling the hot water just enough to make it perfect for bathing. The wind blew gently over us, and the sound of the rushing water was as soothing as the warmth. The mountain loomed above us with the last cloudy remains of the thunderstorm hovering at the top.

I still hadn't found the perfect place in the pool. The hot water hitting my back was a little too hot for my tastes, but my toes, encased in water shoes to help me navigate the stony bottom of the pool, were caught in the current of the Gardner and felt like ice.

"Move over," I said to Cooper, forcing him to float down a few feet until I found the perfect mixture of hot and cold water. I gripped the rock beside me lazily as the current tried to carry me downstream. This was the life! Much better than thunderstorms and ghost trains that ran on invisible tracks and vanished into the storm. I closed my eyes and relaxed.

"One more day in Yellowstone," Cooper called from downstream. "What do you want to do?"

My eyes jerked open, and I stared at the cloudy mountain peak far above me. "I do not want to visit another ghost town!" I said fervently. "Let's drive down to Old Faithful and hike around the Upper Geyser Basin."

"Works for me," said Cooper as he settled deeper into the warm water.

8

Thirty-Seven Days

CRESCENT HILL

Prologue

He was a nearsighted widower of fifty-four years when the Washburn Expedition was announced. He was a townsman by choice, with no wilderness experience, but he'd been intrigued by the reports of the Yellowstone region and wanted to see this magnificent wonderland among the wild Rocky Mountains for himself. So he finagled his way onto the expedition and headed south toward Yellowstone.

Early in the trip, he fell sick from eating too many wild berries and was left behind at Bottler's ranch in Pleasant Valley. But he recovered within two days and swiftly caught up with the expedition, which was traveling up the mighty canyon of the Yellowstone.

On dark nights when the wolves howled and the stars twinkled brightly in the September sky, the expedition members sat around the fire and discussed what they should do if any member became separated from the group. After much debate, the group decided that a man lost during this leg of their journey should make for the hot springs on the southwest arm of Yellowstone Lake—around which they were traversing—and wait for the expedition to join him. The townsman was not pleased with this decision. He thought a lost man should head due west, locate the Madison River, and follow it back to the settlements. But his suggestion was overruled. At the time, it seemed like a philosophical debate to pass the time. Nothing could possibly happen to him.

He was wrong.

Days 1–4

When the expedition reached the southern peninsula of the lake, their way was impeded by an impenetrable pine forest with so many logs piled on top of one another that the terrain was nearly impassable. As the expedition sought a way through the massive tangle, the townsman became separated from the group. He was unalarmed. Short separations regularly occurred among the group. But darkness encroached before he located anyone, so he picketed his horse, built a fire, and went to sleep.

In the morning, he turned north toward Yellowstone Lake, hoping to find his companions camped on the lakeshore. The way was slower than ever, with dense forest and fallen logs impeding every step. He dismounted to look through a promising gap in the forest, hoping it led to an easy trail. In that moment, his horse spooked and galloped away, carrying the townsman's blankets, guns, fishing tackle, and matches with him. He raced after his horse, hoping to retrieve it. After a half-day of tramping over rocks, ridges, small streams, and too many darned fallen trees, he realized his horse was gone for good. The townsman was all alone in the wilderness with two knives, a small opera glass, and the clothes he stood up in.

After a hunger-filled night, the townsman headed for the planned meeting place by the hot springs on the southwest arm of Yellowstone Lake. Weak with hunger, he scrambled over rocks and fallen trees until he broke out upon the shores of a lovely lake glittering in the sunbeams. Framed by lofty mountains, the lake curved enticingly away from him as he staggered onto the sandy beach. Steam rose from nearby hot springs, and a small geyser bubbled a cheerful greeting to the weary traveler. This was not the massive Yellowstone Lake he sought. He must have gotten turned around.

The hungry townsman sank down on a rock and searched the bucolic scene for signs of a rescue party. He saw otters playing in the water and elk grazing along the lake edge, but no sign of men or horses. For a moment, he buried his face in his hands in despair. Then he spotted an elk thistle with an edible root. Food! He'd found food. The townsman pulled it from the ground and ate the long taper in a few bites. Much cheered, he lay down under a slender tree to rest.

The townsman was awakened in the night by the scream of a mountain lion. He levitated himself into the branches of the tree above, terror giving him a strength he did not normally possess. He shouted at the creature and rattled the branches, trying to frighten it away. The mountain lion paced around the base of the tree, screaming back at him. He broke pieces from the branches and pelted the snarling beast as it snuffled and pawed at the tree, seeking a way up. Finally, the townsman wrapped his arms around the trunk and went completely still, trying to fool the beast into thinking he'd escaped. For several tense moments, the mountain lion continued snuffling and pacing around the base of the tree. Then the creature gave an angry screech and plunged away into the underbrush. When he was sure the lion was gone, the townsman slid to the ground and fell into a deep slumber that lasted well past daylight.

Days 5–13

In the morning, a rain-and-snowstorm rolled over the lakeshore. The townsman lay under a spruce tree, covered with earth and boughs to keep out the worst of the cold. On the second day of the storm, an unwary songbird hopped into his meager shelter and became a raw meal for the starving man.

During a lull, he trudged around the lake on frostbitten feet, determined to reach the hot cauldrons on the far side. He chose a place between two hot springs to build a small shelter made of branches and lined it with fallen foliage to sleep upon. He lay quietly in this bower during the three-day storm. Steam swooshed over him from the hot pools on either side until he felt parboiled. On the third day, he turned in his sleep and broke a hole through the thin ground. Hot steam poured from the hole, severely burning his hip. He was forced to wait four days more for his wound to heal sufficiently so that he could travel. He spend the wait time creating pouches to carry the thistles he harvested and teaching himself to make a fire using his travel opera glass.

Days 14–19

He tried to make his way back toward Yellowstone Lake in the morning, but night found him on a bleak hillside with no fire and no shelter. He walked constantly back and forth during the dark hours, banging his hands and feet against logs to keep from freezing to death. The next morning, he returned to the little lake to build a fire on the shore and recover some strength.

He stocked up on thistles while reviewing his plans. The expedition would have given him up for dead by now, so he must make his own way home. He could retrace the expedition's path around the huge lake and back up the Yellowstone River or follow the plan he'd favored when the expedition discussed the options for a lost man. He disliked the idea of retracing his steps, so decided to head westward toward the Madison Mountains.

When he left in the morning, the townsman carried a small brand of fire with him so as not to be caught again unsheltered from the cold. He trudged through thickets and dense forest, eating thistle roots for sustenance. The exercise inflamed his burned hip, and he was forced to sleep sitting up. That night, darkness crowded close around him; every puff of wind an evil voice, every glimmer the eyes of a crouching monster, every lonely howl a ravening wolf pack. When he finally dozed off, the townsman fell into the fire, burning himself yet again.

The townsman arrived on the shores of Yellowstone Lake late the next afternoon. In the morning, he located the abandoned expedition camp in the hot springs basin on the southwestern arm of the lake. They'd obviously stayed at the hot springs for many days, hoping he would make his way to them. The townsman searched the camp in vain for a written message or supplies. In his inexperience, he did not realize that the supplies left behind by the expedition had been cached to keep them safe from bears.

Deciding to follow the expedition's trail out of Yellowstone, the townsman camped that night beneath a bower of branches to shelter from the cold wind blowing off the lake. He awoke to find his shelter burning and a fire raging through the trees behind him. Escaping the blaze, he huddled on the lakeshore, watching the forest burn spectacularly before his eyes. Assessing his wounds in the morning, he found his hair scorched closer than a barber's haircut and his left hand severely burned.

Days 20–23

All trace of the expedition was obliterated by the forest fire, so the townsman headed west, hoping to find a pass through the Madison Mountain Range. He had eaten the last of the thistle roots and traveled in a daze of hunger through a rough and jagged land; climbing tall ridges, roaming through rugged hills, and clambering over wind fallen piles of dead timber.

By the second day of his westward journey, the townsman was in despair. The still-distant mountains loomed jagged and threatening before him. How would he find a pass through such behemoths? As he sat staring at his mountain nemesis, a glowing specter appeared before him, its feet hovering just above the ground. The townsman gaped in shock, recognizing the figure as an old clerical friend who had been dead for many years.

"Go back immediately, as rapidly as your strength will permit," the ghost told him. "There is no food here, and the idea of scaling these rocks is madness."

"Doctor," he rejoined, "the distance is too great. I cannot live to travel it."

"Say not so," replied his friend. "Your life depends upon the effort. Return at once. Start now, lest your resolution falter. Travel as fast and as far as possible—it is your only chance."

"My shoes are nearly worn, my clothes are in tatters. My strength is almost overcome," the townsman wailed. "As a last trial, it seems to me I can but attempt to scale this mountain or perish in the effort, if God so wills."

"Don't think of it," said his ghostly advisor. "Your power of endurance will carry you through. I will accompany you. Put your trust in heaven. Help yourself and God will help you."

And so the townsman turned around and struggled for the next two days back toward Yellowstone Lake. He came at last to the place in the north where the Yellowstone River exited the lake. There, fatigued nearly to death, he found some thistles and ate for the first time in four days.

Days 24–37

He lost all track of time after reaching the river. He vaguely remembered seeing the great waterfalls in the immense canyon as he sat beside a small fire, trying to warm his right arm, paralyzed after a bitter cold night. He recalled catching some minnows that made him sick. He recollected luscious dreams filled with feasts at the finest restaurants in New York and Washington. And he rather thought that he slept one night in the den of a bear. He woke in the morning to find his campfire had burned the woods all around him, chasing off the den's former occupant.

He hallucinated constantly. His stomach and his arms and his legs took on the guise of imaginary companions that complained bitterly at his treatment of them and forced him to do things like eat and walk and pick up firewood. After he passed Tower Falls, he stumbled out into a wasteland filled with unsheltered meadows, sagebrush, stunted trees, barren hillsides, and ravines filled with rocky debris. He was still many miles from the ranch where he'd recovered from his berry-induced illness, and he didn't think he could make it that far. Still he stumbled onward; sleeping in sagebrush, losing and finding the

THIRTY-SEVEN DAYS

precious glass that gave him fire, clambering from rocky shelter to rocky shelter.

And then one bitter cold morning as he groped along the side of Crescent Hill, he looked up into the compassionate eyes of Yellowstone Jack Baronett, who said, "Are you Truman Everts?" The lost had been found.

Epilogue

At the time he was rescued, Truman Everts was an emaciated, unshaven skeleton weighing approximately fifty pounds. Yellowstone Jack found him crawling on his hands and feet, delirious with cold and exposure. His clothes were in rags, bones protruded through the skin on his feet and thighs, and his fingers were shaped like bird claws. He didn't look human.

Everts spent many days recuperating after his ordeal—first at the campfire of the two mountain men sent to search for him and later succored at the cabin of two miners. The miners healed his wounded stomach with bear-fat oil and then fed him and tended his wounds. By the time the ambulance arrived from Fort Ellis to fetch him, he was well on his way to recovery.

Everts wrote about his hair-raising adventure in a story titled "Thirty-Seven Days of Peril" published the next year in *Scribner's Monthly*. He became a celebrated figure throughout the country and was asked if he would become the very first superintendent of the newly created Yellowstone National Park—an honor he refused.

Everts married for the second time at the age of sixty-four and fathered a son he named Truman Everts Jr. According to his son, the burn on Everts's left hand—received during the massive forest fire at West Thumb—pained him until his death at age eighty-five.

9

The Drowned Man

STEVENSON ISLAND

My supervisor called me just after sunrise on a warm summer morning in 1929 to report another incident aboard the shipwrecked *E.C. Waters* out on Stevenson Island.

"A bunch of drunks were boozing and brawling on the boat last night," he said in a grumpy tone that clearly indicated his lack of morning coffee.

I sighed. Again! I had no idea why so many summer visitors flocked to the wreck of the old steamboat on Stevenson Island, which lay partially submerged beside a sandy beach. In its heyday, the derelict tour boat stretched 125 feet stem to stern and had room for five hundred passengers. Its reported cost was sixty thousand dollars, a huge sum in 1905. The new steamboat was by far the largest ship ever on the lake and seemed to promise financial success for its owner and namesake, E. C. Waters, who ran the much-maligned Yellowstone Lake Boat Company from 1891 to 1907.

Waters was an old reprobate with a bad reputation who ran a leaky fleet of rowboats and a steamship that ferried park visitors from West Thumb up to Lake Hotel. He stuffed his boats with more passengers than they could safely hold. He charged folks a fee upon boarding the boat and another upon exiting. He also charged folks to visit his little menagerie on Dot Island, which featured elk, bison, and other native animals. Waters severely neglected his creatures, and complaints grew so numerous that he was forced to shut down this side venture. Indeed, E. C. Waters's actions were so unethical that the park threw him out in 1907. In revenge, the thwarted entrepreneur guided his namesake steamship out to Stevenson Island, shot up its hull, and left it moored there to rot.

At first, the abandoned steamboat withstood the steady battering of Yellowstone Lake's wind, waves, ice, and snow. But when the ice broke up in 1921, the ship was pushed onto the beach. In 1926, the steam boiler that drove the engine was removed and used to heat the Lake Hotel. Winter skiers that ventured across the frozen lake started using the derelict ship as a warming hut, and it became a prop for Jack Croney's fish-fry business as well as a retreat for brawls fueled with moonshine, like the one last night.

"I want you to head out to the island and make sure no one got stranded there when the brawl ended," my supervisor continued.

"Right, boss," I said.

I reckoned it wasn't much fun to wake up after an all-night drinking party and find yourself stranded on an island in the middle of Yellowstone Lake. Such a person would be tempted to swim for shore, which was the last thing the park needed. The water in Yellowstone Lake was pretty frigid at the best of times, averaging 41 degrees Fahrenheit when not completely frozen. It only took twenty minutes for hypothermia to kick in at those low temperatures. Folks that went down in Yellowstone Lake didn't tend to come up.

THE DROWNED MAN

I hurried down to the marina and headed out in the boat we used for official business. It was a short ride out to Stevenson Island. I sighed as I drew closer to the creaky old tub listing precariously on the shore. There were empty beer bottles strewn on the beach and floating in the water, always a sign of trespassers. I moored my craft and gathered up as much trash as I could. Then I cautiously ventured onto the rickety steamboat. It reeked of rotting wet wood, urine, and stale alcohol. I held my nose as I searched from stem to stern for intruders in the creaking, swaying mess. The floor was so sticky with spilled moonshine that dead leaves and shredded bottle labels adhered to my boots. My feet crunched on splintered glass where several bottles had broken. Yuck. I shouted a couple of times, but no one answered and I found no bodies huddled asleep in the wreck. Time to check the island.

Stevenson Island was the second largest island in Yellowstone Lake. It was 1.3 miles long, and I was going to have to check the whole darn thing, just in case some of the drunks had gone exploring last night. With a sigh, I headed out in a basic search pattern, keeping my eyes peeled for any stranded brawlers along the sandy beaches or in the interior where trees and bracken grew. My only company was a light summer breeze that tickled my neck. The sun glittered on still, serene water. At least I had a lovely morning for my search.

By mid-morning, I was hot, grumpy, tired, and convinced I was on a wild-goose chase. There had been no sign of visitors. If any of the brawlers had been stranded on the island, they were long gone by now. I headed back toward the sunlit beach, ready to return to the mainland.

As I came over a tiny rise, the sun disappeared suddenly, as if a giant hand had clamped over it. A huge gust of wind

struck me hard, making me stagger backward a few paces. The
wind was strangely cold for a day that had started out warm and
sunny. In front of me, I saw the lake churning in great waves
while a storm cloud massed overhead. My heart pounded with
sudden fear. It would not be easy navigating back to land in
these conditions.

Then I saw something big and bulky floating at the edge
of the water. Something man-shaped. My heart leapt into my
throat, and I rushed forward with a strangled cry. Dear God,
someone *had* tried to swim to shore and drowned. Or maybe
the person had fallen from the boat last night and hit his or her
head. My hands felt cold and clammy as I fumbled for the kit
in my backpack, my mind racing with the list of things I'd been
trained to do in an emergency situation.

I broke through the last of the bracken and leapt onto the
beach. The storm wind nearly blew me over. I pressed forward,
clothes flapping. My hat went flying and I grabbed it just in
time. The temperature on the beach was below freezing. I could
see my breath as I ran toward the still figure lying half on and
half off the sand.

As I dropped to my knees beside the body, I noticed that
the sodden clothing was old-fashioned, dating from long
before the Great War. The drowned man looked rather like
a fur trapper or explorer from the era when Yellowstone was
first discovered. Very strange. Green weeds were caught on the
sleeve of the man's waterlogged coat and in his ragged wet hair.
I checked his neck for a pulse. None. I turned the body over.
The corpse felt ice-cold as I performed other checks to see if
life was still present. I stared into a pair of bulging brown eyes
on a blue-white face. He'd been awake when he died. Looking

at the distended body, I wasn't sure if the death verdict would be hypothermia or drowning—or both. The man looked rather frostbitten. He was fairly young, his hair dark and his bearded face unlined.

I swallowed back nausea. No amount of training ever prepares you for your first death. Though my instincts informed me there was no reviving this long-dead corpse. *I'd better do this by the book*, I decided.

Fighting for control of my stomach, I took a deep breath and bent over the body. In between one breath and the next, it vanished. My hand was still outstretched, but suddenly it gripped empty air instead of an old-fashioned jacket. I reeled backward with a gasp and landed on my rump in the sand. Where had the corpse gone?

I glanced frantically over the calm, sparkling waters of the still lake, searching for the body of the drowned man. The warm summer wind caressed my face as my brain registered the change in scenery. What had happened to the approaching storm? Where were the huge, wind-swept swells that had frightened me so much when I came over the rise?

I scrambled to my feet and stood hyperventilating with my head between my legs, arms braced on my knees. This couldn't be happening. But I knew it was. Storm, winter cold, and corpse had vanished in a heartbeat. They had been shades of a former time, a former accident. So *that* was why the man's clothes had been so old-fashioned.

I slowly pushed myself upright, wondering what—if anything—I should report to my supervisor. I couldn't tell him I'd seen a ghost! He'd fire me. To tell the truth, I wasn't sure I hadn't been hallucinating. I was a scientific man and I didn't believe in ghosts or the supernatural. But I had no other term for what I'd just seen.

Spooked by the incident, I felt an urgent need to walk the perimeter of the island one more time, searching the waters intently for any sign of a drowning victim. I found nothing but a flock of white pelicans feeding peacefully near the wreck of the *E.C. Waters.*

Finally I unmoored the official park boat and leapt in, glad to get away from Stevenson Island. Folks said that Yellowstone Lake never gave up its dead. Apparently, neither did the island.

I turned my craft and expertly navigated through the sparkling waters of Yellowstone Lake as the white pelicans flapped lazily away overhead.

10

The Ghost in Room 203

FOUNTAIN FLATS

The summer employee did not want to leave Yellowstone at the end of the season, so he applied for a job as winter keeper at the Fountain Hotel. The elite hotel—which opened in 1891—sat on a small rise in Fountain Flats, close to the Fountain Paint Pots. The view of the geyser basin was magnificent and the hot springs were virtually right outside the door.

The employee was overjoyed when his application was accepted. The winter work at the hotel would be minimal. And his close acquaintance with the soldiers stationed at Fort Mammoth meant that he'd have company to break up his long winter evenings. If he ever grew bored—which was unlikely—there was the endless display of the fountain basin geysers and mud pots just outside his door to entertain him. Not to mention the wildlife that came down from the mountains to graze near the heated pools.

Only a handful of guests—the last of the season—were staying at the hotel when the first ghostly incident occurred in Room 203. The caretaker was working behind the counter at 6:00 p.m., and darkness had fallen when the call bell rang for Room 203. The caretaker was surprised. No one was staying in Room 203. Who had rung the bell? He hurried upstairs, wondering if he'd given one of the guests the wrong room key. He knocked on the door and called out. No answer.

Using the master key, he opened the door and stepped inside. The room was empty. He blinked in astonishment and felt goose bumps rise on his arms and legs. This was . . . strange. The caretaker closed the door in a hurry and returned to his desk duties.

The final guests of the season checked out in the morning, and most of the hotel staff followed suit, leaving only one man to help the caretaker close the hotel for the winter. There was a great deal of work to do, but the caretaker rather enjoyed having the place to himself with no guests to cater to. The luxurious feeling lasted until six o'clock that night, when the call bell for Room 203 tinkled happily into the echoing emptiness of the lobby.

"What the dickens?" the caretaker exclaimed, rearing up out of his seat.

"Is that the call bell?" his colleague called from the kitchen. "I thought all the guests were gone."

"They are," the caretaker said.

Mad as blazes at whoever was pulling such a prank, he marched upstairs to Room 203. Knocking and entering at the same time, the caretaker flicked on the light, ready to ream out the jokester hiding behind the door. No one was there. He checked under the bed. Nothing. He looked out the window to see if anyone had climbed in from outside, but there was no rope or ladder present. He retreated, more than a little spooked. Who had rung the call bell?

His colleague came out of the kitchen to inquire about the bell, but the caretaker didn't have a satisfactory answer. "Probably one of the staff playing tricks on you," he opined.

"I don't see how, unless they can scale a wall without a rope," the caretaker replied. Still, the idea comforted him.

The caretaker was washing the windows in the lobby the next evening when the call bell rang for Room 203. His colleague was away on an errand, so he was alone in the building—or so he thought. He glanced at the clock and saw that it was exactly six o'clock. He fetched a heavy paperweight from the counter before climbing the stairs to the second floor. He wasn't prepared to face . . . whatever it was . . . without some kind of weapon.

The caretaker turned the key in the lock and swung the door open with a mighty crash, hoping to scare the prankster. The room was dark and silent in the chill autumn night. He flicked on the light switch, and the room flooded with light. It was empty. He glanced under the bed. Nothing. "Who's there?" he called into the stillness. His voice sounded too loud in the bright, empty room. His words echoed back at him in a low-pitched and menacing tone: "Who's there?"

The caretaker backed out of the room, and the door slammed shut. He raced down the stairs and out the front door. He stood breathing rapidly in the cold twilight, as elk grazed in the field beyond and a coyote yelped in the distance. He lit a cigarette with trembling hands and stood smoking outside until his colleague came back from his errand.

Over dinner, the caretaker told his colleague about the ringing of the call bell and his frightening experience in the room. His colleague said, "Sounds like a ghost to me." Not what the caretaker wanted to hear.

Bright autumn sunshine greeted the men in the morning. There was frost on the ground, and the steam from the hot springs added a lovely dazzle to the day. The caretaker decided that he had been foolish. There had been no ghostly echo in Room 203 last night. The riddle of the call bell could surely be explained in some rational manner. Still, his heart pounded strangely when his colleague bade him farewell at lunchtime. The heavy work was done, and the caretaker could do the rest of the winterizing without assistance.

"Have a good winter," his colleague said cheerfully as he left the hotel. "Don't disturb the ghost in Room 203!"

The caretaker jumped nervously, and his friend pounded him on the shoulder. "Hey, you can handle a little old ghost with one hand tied behind your back."

"I hope so," the caretaker said doubtfully.

He was polishing the countertop when the call bell rang at six o'clock that evening. This time, the caretaker grabbed the pistol from the desk drawer before mounting the steps to the second floor. The hallway felt unnaturally cold, but the caretaker's hands were sweating when he opened the door to Room 203. He stared for a moment into a cold darkness that seemed to writhe as his trembling hand snapped on the light. At once, the empty room came into focus.

The caretaker's legs shook so badly that he could hardly walk. His breath iced in the air before him as he checked under the bed. No one was there. He glanced in the mirror, convinced he'd seen movement behind him. He whirled. Nothing was there. "Come out," he called bravely, his breath a puff of mist before his face. "Come out," the empty room echoed around him. "Come out."

The shadows seemed deeper over by the window. The cold air shimmered before his eyes. "Stop ringing the bell," he

THE GHOST IN ROOM 203

shouted suddenly, holding the pistol up with trembling hands. The room reverberated. The chill deepened.

Snapping off the light, the caretaker ran downstairs and retreated to his rooms, shaking so hard he could hardly stand upright. He vowed that he would not answer the call bell again, no matter how many times it rang. And he kept that promise. Each evening, the call bell for Room 203 sang out its summons at exactly six o'clock, and each evening the caretaker refused to answer it, though his blood ran cold every time it rang.

It was easy to forget the ghost during the day when the caretaker did his chores or wandered through the geyser basin, watching the bison and admiring the yellow aspens. But when six o'clock drew near, the caretaker's feet turned him willy-nilly toward the hotel lobby. He hated the six o'clock call bell, yet he was drawn to it. If the call bell ceased even once to ring out its evening summons, the caretaker would know it was all a joke. But the bell rang every night without fail.

One day, a thought occurred to the caretaker that frightened him even more than the daily call bell: What if the ghost in Room 203 grew angry because he refused to answer its summons? What if the phantom came looking for him?

The caretaker could not shake the thought. He jumped every time the building creaked. He peered into every shadow whenever he entered a room. Chills shook his body every time the local wildlife howled or snorted or hissed outside the hotel. He woke one morning to see a big bull bison peering in the bedroom window and nearly died of a heart attack. Heart pounding, he stared at the huge creature blinking lazily in the sunlight, and he remembered the story of Meeteetse Wahb, the grizzly bear who invaded the lobby of the Fountain Hotel and stole a side of beef from the kitchen while the hotel guests screamed. Maybe he could lure this bison up to Room 203. That would surely take care of the ghost! Or would it? He'd try just about anything to get rid of that darned bell-ringing ghost! The bison walked away before he could decide.

A photographer friend dropped in unexpectedly the next day. Over lunch, the two men discussed the ghost in Room 203. The photographer had learned about the incident down in Old Faithful while closing the inn with the help of the caretaker's former colleague. Intrigued, the photographer had come to the Fountain Hotel to hear the ghostly call bell for himself. Glad of the company, the caretaker invited him to stay the night.

The two men were sitting behind the counter in the empty hotel when the call bell echoed eerily through the lobby at six o'clock. The sound seemed to go on and on. The photographer's eyes grew wide with fright when he heard the phantom ringing. "The ghost," he gasped. "The ghost!" Leaping over the counter in a single bound, he ran into the night.

The caretaker stared after his fleeing friend in astonishment. Then rage overtook his own fear. He sprang to his feet, every nerve fired up. This was the last straw! The ghost had chased off the only company he'd had in weeks. He was *done* with this ghost!

The caretaker ran upstairs, threw open the door to Room 203, and screamed: "All right, you win! You've got the place to yourself from now on. *I hope you're satisfied!*"

Cold air spilled from the night-darkened room, chilling him to the bone. The caretaker thought he smelled grave dust and death in the little breeze that patted his cheeks and tugged his hair. He screamed and kept on screaming as he ran down the stairs and out the front door. He found his photographer friend saddling his horse in the barn.

"Saddle mine too," he said. He raced back to the hotel and packed his bags. The two men camped out on the icy flats that night, building a roaring fire to keep away the wildlife and any supernatural figures that might have followed them from the hotel. In the morning, the caretaker rode to the park office to collect his pay. They'd have to hire someone else to be the winter keeper for the Fountain Hotel. He was done.

Some time later, an old friend from Yellowstone stopped by the ex-caretaker's home for dinner. "They found that ghost of yours," the friend said with a grin as the men ate dessert in front of the fireplace.

The ex-caretaker sat bolt upright in their chair. "They did?" he asked incredulously. "Did they call in an exorcist?"

"They didn't need an exorcist. They needed an exterminator," his friend replied. "When the park had Room 203 renovated, the workers found the call-bell wire stripped of insulation. Apparently, a mouse chewed it off. Whenever the little critter stepped on the bare wire, the bell would ring."

"So you're saying that a mouse—a very small creature not known for its keen intellect—stepped on the call-bell wire *every night* at six on the dot?" the ex-caretaker said sarcastically. "It must have been a very punctual mouse!"

"Well, when you put it like that . . ." the friend began. His voice trailed off and he looked thoughtful.

The ex-caretaker shrugged. He didn't care what the park staff found in the walls. He knew what he'd experienced in Room 203 was the real deal. If the park wanted to believe the spirit in Room 203 was actually a mouse, so be it. It probably sounded better on the official reports.

Rumors of a ghost in the Fountain Hotel continued among the Yellowstone staff until the hotel closed its doors for the last time in 1917. Even today the story lingers. Was the ghost of Room 203 really an intelligent and very punctual mouse? Or was it something else?

11

The Miner's Ghost

COOKE CITY

When I heard there might be gold on the Crow reservation, I packed up my gear, my mule, and my dog, Rex. We headed for the Absaroka Mountains. A few prospectors got to the narrow mountain valley ahead of me and were already panning, but I put up a cabin and started building sluice boxes pretty quick, hoping to strike it rich. I got lucky in the autumn and found me a promising vein of silver just before I had to quit mining to stock up on vittles and cut hay for my mule so we could make it through the winter in my remote cabin.

The snows came down early from the mountains, and they were heavier than any I'd seen before. I had to tunnel my way out to the barn to take care of old Bessie. My cabin was pretty much buried, but the piled-up snow kept it warm and snug.

When spring came, we broke free of the dad-blame snow and I started digging myself a mine, following that vein of silver. I figured I'd be rich by summer, but the silver vein petered out, and it was back to square one for me and old Rex. Meantime, a group of prospectors came to the valley that spring and set up their claim a few miles away. And, gosh-dern it, them prospectors found gold! Jiminy, but I was mad!

75

THE MINER'S GHOST

A feller named Adam Miller filed the first official mining claim in 1871, and the whole area quickly became known as the New World Mining District. I filed my claim right after Miller, nice and official. By then, I'd found a big lead deposit, and it was a sight more profitable than the little silver vein I'd originally pursued. That same year, a feller named Pete filed a claim next to mine and we got friendly. Pete was always hankering after gold, and he fussed about the lack of it whenever we met. Still, he was doing well for himself mining lead, same as me.

Several years slid by in a heartbeat. Suddenly it was June of 1877, and folks in our mining town were all agitated about a band of Nez Perce that had started a war against the white man. The Nez Perce were seeking revenge for crimes against their tribe, including the murder of relatives and the loss of their homeland. Can't say I blamed them for being mad. I'd start a war too if folks killed my family and threw me off my claim. I knew better than to voice my views in the town, though. Folks were real scared.

Pete stopped by my cabin one evening in July with the latest report from the settlements. "I hear the Nez Perce have left the Idaho reservation," he said, setting himself on the wood bench by my front door and lighting his pipe. "A huge band of them are on their way to Montana buffalo country. At least 200 men and about 550 women and children."

"Not good," I said, rubbing old Rex behind the ears.

"Folks in town say the Nez Perce are heading to Crow country. They've got friends among the Crow who might help them fight the army."

I sat bolt upright at this news. Crow country was just over the mountain from here.

"Are you thinking about pulling out?" I asked, feeling my stomach sink at the prospect.

"Heck, no. I'd never leave my claim. Just thought I should warn you," Pete replied.

I was jittery all that night, wondering what I would do if the Nez Perce came through this valley. The warriors had been pretty ruthless to the white settlers living along the Snake. They wouldn't hesitate to kill a miner that lived alone on his claim.

After some thought, I decided to disguise the entrance to my little mine, make it look as if it had been abandoned. I spent several days planting shrubbery and arranging a fallen log in front of the entrance. I even planted sagebrush over the debris piles to make them look overgrown. By the time I finished, the Nez Perce could have walked right past the mine without seeing it. I hoped.

Each morning, I'd move the fallen log to let Bessie in with the rubble wagon. Each evening, I'd put it back, just in case. It was a right pain in the nether regions, but it was better than having my ore stolen by the Nez Perce.

There wasn't much I could do to hide my cabin or Bessie's stable, so I carved a hidey-hole inside the mine with a rock cover to disguise it and put my fiddle and the spare rifle and the box containing Mama's wedding ring on a high shelf inside. Then I hollowed out a stable for Bessie and moved a stack of hay inside. The animals and I would retreat to the mine if the Nez Perce raided this region on their way to the Crow reservation.

On August first, the ground shook from the force of an explosion over on Pete's claim, followed by the ear-splitting roar of falling rock. Quicker than lightning, I unhitched Bessie from the mine wagon and rode the mule over to Pete's place to make sure he was all right. Pete's mine had been buried by a massive stone avalanche. I looked around for Pete and saw the toe of one boot sticking out from underneath a boulder. I rode lickety-split to town to get help. It took six men to shift that boulder, and Pete's body was broken and bleeding when we got it out. We buried Pete behind his cabin and said a few words over his body. It was real sad.

A few days later, US soldiers staged a surprise attack against the Nez Perce encampment at the Big Hole River. The newspapers reported sixty Nez Perce dead, mostly women and children, and twenty-five US casualties, with another thirty-eight soldiers wounded. Sentiment was running high against the Nez Perce, who were attacking ranches and freight teamsters as they fled toward Yellowstone. Everyone in the region was in a panic, and the newspapers were fanning the flames.

By late August, the Nez Perce had entered West Yellowstone and were slowly making their way toward the Madison and Firehole Rivers. I carried my gun everywhere, and all my valuables were in the hidey-hole way back in the mine.

When I brought Bessie to town for shoeing, the blacksmith told me that nine people had been captured in a Yellowstone tourist party, and ten in another. He was thinking about sending his wife back east to stay with her family until the danger had passed. I couldn't blame him. A few days later, we learned that all but two of the Yellowstone tourists were freed or managed to escape, suffering minor wounds.

Everyone in town was in a tizzy by now. Rumors flew around the mining camp. The Nez Perce were heading up the old Bannock trail. The Nez Perce were in Pelican Creek, heading toward the Lamar River. A hysterical teamster came barreling into town one morning to report that a rearguard of Nez Perce warriors had run into more Yellowstone tourists and had killed two of them. "And they burned a ranch," he added, crossing himself with his hat.

After hearing this news, folks in town that had families to care for closed up shop and hustled their loved ones to safety. The rest of us loaded up on ammo and stayed on our claims, ready to fight. I moved old Rex and Bessie into the disguised mine along with all our vittles and bedding. Then I tossed leaves around the cabin floor and blocked the chimney with sagebrush to make it look as if I'd abandoned my claim. Best to lie low until the danger passed.

After a few tense days in hiding, I ran out of tobacco and coffee—two essential ingredients for survival, at least in my book. Leaving Bessie in her shaft stall, Rex and I headed down to the general store to stock up on supplies. The crowd in the store was filled with good cheer. The latest word was the Nez Perce were heading toward Clark's Fork Canyon with General Howard hot on their trail.

"They wanted to avoid us tough miners," boasted the shopkeeper. "They knew we could take 'em."

Sure we could. That's why everyone panicked, I thought, shaking my head over the follies of mankind. I bought supplies and headed home with old Rex at my heels.

As I drew near my cabin, Pete's ghost appeared abruptly in front of me with a faint popping noise like a cork coming out of a bottle. The air swirled around as if he stood in the midst of a windstorm. Some of the swirling air flowed over me, chilling my skin and making old Rex growl nervously. I stared at Pete with my mouth hanging open, instinctively raising my rifle. Not that it would do me any good against a ghost. The setting sun was shining right through Pete's body, and I realized with a twang of terror that his feet were a good six inches above the ground.

"Get into the mine *right now!*" Pete exclaimed. "A Nez Perce scouting party is setting fire to my old cabin over the ridge. They'll be over here in a moment. Run!"

It took a moment for his words to register in my flabbergasted mind. The Nez Perce were coming! Great God in Heaven!

"Thanks, Pete," I gasped and ran like the devil with my dog at my heels.

We slid through the bracken-covered entrance, leapt into the hidey-hole, and rolled the concealing rock into place. In the darkness of her makeshift stable, I heard Bessie munching on her hay. Then war whoops resounded over the ridge. Nez Perce warriors galloped into my cabin clearing with gunshots and shouts of triumph. Wood smashed as they raided my house, and I smelled fire burning. I swallowed and stroked old Rex to keep him calm.

All at once, I heard the warriors talking outside the mine. I clutched my rifle when I heard the scrape of the fallen log as it was moved away from the entrance. Footsteps echoed down the main passage. *They'll see Bessie and know that we're here*, I thought in alarm. I grabbed the concealing rock with my free hand, ready to push it aside and start shooting. Then I sensed Pete's presence in the hidey-hole with us. His hand touched my shoulder, calming me.

"Wait," he whispered. I waited. The footsteps hesitated at the fork between the main shaft and a side tunnel that exited on the far side of the mountain. After a heart-stopping moment of consideration, the warriors turned down the side tunnel, away from Bessie and our hidey-hole. Five minutes later, the Nez Perce exited the mine and regrouped with their companions. I heard them ride away.

"Well done," Pete said, his voice echoing through the hidey-hole. His hand squeezed my shoulder once more. Then Rex and I were alone.

Belatedly, Bessie panicked at the smell of smoke from the burning cabin. I calmed her before she injured herself and went outside to see if there was anything left of my property. A short cloudburst doused the worst of the fire, but I'd have to completely rebuild the barn. Still, we were all alive, which was the important thing.

The Nez Perce tracks exited southeast in the direction of Dead Indian Hill, so I assumed the scouts had decided to rejoin their tribe at Clark's Fork. In the morning, I heard that the Nez Perce scouts were accused of burning the gold mills and stealing a shipment of silver bullion.

I lost nothing of value in the unexpected raid, thanks to Pete's ghost. While I rebuilt my cabin and barn, the Nez Perce—rejected by their friends among the Crow—made a run for Canada. A final battle near the Bear's Paw Mountains held off US troops long enough for sixty women, eight children, and 103 men to slip across the border and live among the Sioux under Sitting Bull, who had been there since the Little Big Horn campaign the year before. The rest surrendered with Chief Joseph on October 5, 1877. The Nez Perce war was over.

12

Double or Nothing

NORRIS

It was mighty cold that April of 1904, and one of our fellow soldiers—Private Richard Hurley of Company F, Third Cavalry—fell ill with dysentery at the Snake Station on the south border of Yellowstone National Park. Old Joe, as we called him, wasn't looking so hot. He lost weight right quick, 'til he resembled a walking skeleton. It frightened Major Sam Martin so much that he bundled up the private and sent a group of us to escort him to Fort Yellowstone in Mammoth for treatment. We stopped at the West Thumb emergency cabin for the night, and by the morning Old Joe had passed. It was very sad.

Figuring the Army would want the private buried in the Mammoth cemetery, we pressed onward through the snow and ice, hauling Old Joe along with us. His corpse got plenty stiff and frozen on the way north, and he resembled an icicle by the time we reached the station at Norris. The living members of our little troop felt nearly as cold as Old Joe. We carried him into the station and set about warming ourselves, building up the fire and cooking up some supper to ease the hunger pangs.

Someone, I think it was Harry, hauled out the whiskey after dinner. "What's say we play some poker, boys?" he called, filling the glasses. His suggestion was met with approval all around. There was nothing like a bit of whiskey to warm the spirits. It felt a bit sacrilege to me to be playing poker while Old Joe lay dead and frozen in the corner, but none of the other fellows seemed to mind. Harry dealt the cards, and we bellied up to the table to play the first round.

The fire barely seemed to keep the spring chill at bay. We kept our jackets on and shivered our way through the first and second hands. Billy won the first and Scotty won the second. I was forced to fold both times. I think it was because I had a hard time keeping my eyes off the corpse in the corner.

Harry was the first one to notice my preoccupation. He studied me surreptitiously during the third round, and by the time I folded my hand, he'd figured out what was wrong. He took a swig of whiskey and gave me a sly grin. "We'd better let Old Joe play a hand," he said. As I gaped incredulously at him, Harry dropped his cards on the table and swaggered across the room to the corner where Private Hurley lay frozen in death. Dragging the body over to the wall by the card table, Harry propped it up against the window.

"Deal," he said to me with a wicked grin. Swallowing, I dealt the cards, adding an extra hand for Old Joe. Harry picked up the cards, spread them a little, and then put them into Old Joe's frozen fingers, forcing the elbows to bend so it looked like old Joe was carefully examining his hand. It looked true to life, since the private had died with his eyes open.

I wasn't the only one sending wary looks Old Joe's way after that. The whole poker game took on an air of bravado that barely covered our uneasiness. No one liked playing poker with a dead man, not even Harry. But no one wanted to admit it, so

DOUBLE OR NOTHING

we played on, drinking whiskey like water to keep up our nerve. By three in the morning, all of us had won several hands and the pile in the middle of the table was getting larger. By dawn, Scotty was down five dollars, Billy was down three, and Harry and I kept trading money back and forth.

Bill and Scott were determined to keep playing until they won their money back, and none of us was eager to go back out into the frigid air, so we dealt another hand. And then another. It was ten in the morning when Harry said, "We'd better wrap it up, boys. They'll be expecting us at the fort sometime today." That was easy for him to say. Harry'd won the pot. Again.

"We've got time for one more game," I said. I was down by a dollar, and I wanted it back. "Double or nothing." Bill and Scott clamored agreement. So Harry dealt out the last hand.

We were studying our cards, ready to place final bids, when we were startled by a flicker of movement in the window. Poor dead Joe stood silhouetted in the morning sunlight, studying the hand we'd dealt him the night before. As we stared at the frozen private, his hands lowered and he placed his cards face up on the table. There was a split second of sheer horror. Then four chairs hit the floorboards simultaneously. Bill and Scott got stuck in the doorway, and I pushed them through and leapt past them into the glittering April snow. Harry kept on running until he reached the edge of the trees, then crouched with his head between his knees, panting with fear.

"He . . . he's alive," Scott gasped, face whiter than the sparkling snow.

"Don't be daft. Old Joe hasn't breathed or had a pulse in three days," Bill said, glancing toward the window where a black figure still loomed by the card table.

"He's a ghost then," Scott said. "Something! You saw him lay down that hand."

I glanced from the two men to the figure in the window, my mind racing. It was a fair morning and the warm sun was making the icicles drip onto the snow below. "He's melting," I said suddenly, and both men turned to look at me.

"Who's melting?" asked Harry, staggering up to join us on legs that still trembled.

"Old Joe. He's not resurrected or a ghost or anything. He's melting in the warm sunlight and his arms unfolded. That's all," I said firmly, hoping to convince myself as well as the others.

"Sounds reasonable," said Scott in a doubtful tone, staring at the dark shadow in the window. I notice he didn't volunteer to go back in the cabin to check.

"I dunno," said Bill darkly. "It was a pretty big pot. And we were playing double or nothing. His ghost probably wanted in on the game."

"Don't be daft," I threw Bill's words back at him. "Old Joe just melted in the sunshine. Come on, let's go back inside. It's bloody cold out here."

I shoved the reluctant soldiers toward the door of the station, unable to resist taking a swift, uneasy glance at the shadow in the window. I figured it would be better not to mention that Joe had a full house when he laid down his hand. He'd probably won the pot, if anyone was fool enough to check. No one did, though. We split the pot equally, collected the private's body with exaggerated care and respect, and headed for Fort Yellowstone a bit faster than was safe in all that snow. Or perhaps even a little faster than that. This was one corpse we wanted off our hands as soon as possible!

13

Dark Presence

CODY

They wanted the house as soon as they saw it. Her husband loved the wide-open spaces of the West and the stories of Buffalo Bill. She loved the proximity of Yellowstone National Park. Their son happily eyed the pretty daughter of the next-door neighbor. It was a perfect place to live. The realtor told them that the stone circles near the property were traces left from a tipi encampment long ago. The circles add a wonderful Western touch to this lovely home. Or so she thought at the time.

The family moved in right away and their son transferred to the local high school. On weekends, the couple cheered their son on at his sporting events, took scenic drives, and visited Yellowstone.

Time passed swiftly, and the son graduated from high school and college, then moved away from home. Empty-nesters now, the husband spent most weekends riding his motorcycle while the wife stayed home and baked.

She was baking blueberry muffins when the hospital called and told her to come at once. Her husband had been in a

DARK PRESENCE

serious accident on his motorcycle. She was out the door in two minutes and raced recklessly to the hospital, hoping to get there in time to say goodbye to her husband.

Someone was waiting for her at the entrance to the emergency room, and she was rushed to her husband's side. There was barely time for him to squeeze her hand and smile into her tear-filled eyes. "Love you, beautiful," he said, and died. It was the worst moment of her life.

Her son arrived soon afterward and drove her home. He took over the funeral arrangements while she wept and finished making the blueberry muffins—her husband's favorite.

The next few days went by in a haze. The house felt empty without her husband, in spite of the friends and family that filled it. And the dog seemed to go mad. He barked and growled whenever anyone opened the door to the cellar, and he refused to go into the den where the family kept his bed.

Soon—too soon—her husband was laid to rest in the local graveyard. Everyone left, including her son, who was packing up his apartment so he could live with her until she grew accustomed to widowhood.

The moment she walked into the empty house, she knew something was wrong. She stood frozen in the living room doorway as the dog came up to her, tail wagging. The dog stopped abruptly and stared into the empty living room, growling softly. His eyes followed the path of . . . something evil . . . that was moving across the floor. Boards creaked under invisible pressure as the . . . something evil . . . entered the den. She watched in terror as the door to the den swung shut of its own volition. The dog barked once, low and fierce, hair spiked up along its back. She shrieked and ran to her bedroom, dog at her heels.

Inside the bedroom, the feeling of malice abated. She knew at once that the Dark Presence could not enter this room. When her eyes fell on the icon of Mary and Baby Jesus hanging on the wall, she understood why: The holy object was generations old, and it glowed faintly in the dimness, its goodness actively pushing back evil.

She sat on the bed and tried to think, the scary scene replaying itself in her mind. Her dog refused to enter the den after her husband's death. Why? *Because it overlooked the tipi ruins.* The thought lodged in her head out of nowhere. She wondered if this house was built on some native burial ground. If so, why hadn't they felt the evil spirit when they first bought the house? Had her husband's presence kept it at bay? Or had it been sleeping until aroused by her terrible grief? She had no answer to these questions.

She kept the dog with her that night. He slept at the foot of the bed, and she was grateful for his snoring presence.

Daylight woke her. She lay sleepily in bed, trying to decide if she should rise. Then she remembered the strange presence in the house last night and sat bolt upright, body cold with fear. "I'm being ridiculous," she told the dog, who was dancing impatiently at the door.

They entered the hall together, and at once she knew she hadn't imagined the Dark Presence. The house seethed with malice. She hurried into the kitchen, where the sense of menace seemed weaker in the dancing sunlight, and let the dog outside to do his business.

As she drank her coffee, her eye fell on the cellar door. The dog had barked and growled whenever someone opened it. Was the Dark Presence in the cellar too? Her hand shook suddenly, splashing coffee on the table, when she remembered that she had a load of laundry in the dryer. She would have to go down in the basement to remove it. She took a deep breath. There was *no way* she was going into the cellar alone.

When the dog finished eating, she put on his leash. He started growling when she opened the cellar door. A flood of cold air rushed over them both. The dog barked sharply as she snapped on the cellar light and gazed down the empty staircase.

"We have to get the laundry," she said, grabbing his collar as she placed her foot on the first step. The dog growled again and showed all his teeth. He backed away, pulling her away with him, and she followed with relief. She sensed a wall of evil at the bottom of the steps, and she did not want to cross it. Better to buy new clothes than go down into that cellar.

She hurried to her room to shower and dress. She wasn't going to spend any more time in this empty house than was strictly necessary. The dog padded into the living room and jumped on the sofa, which she took as a sign that the Dark Presence wasn't in there at the moment. Thank God.

She went to the store to get groceries, then spent the afternoon with a friend who was a grief counselor. She heard the dog barking as soon as she pulled into the driveway at supper time. The dog scraped frantically at the front door as she turned the key and shot into the yard when she opened the door, tail between his legs. He circled the yard several times before he calmed down enough to do his business. She waited for the dog on the doorstep, and they went into the house side by side. She took one shuddering look into the dark living room and swerved into the bright kitchen.

A radio tuned to a Christian station kept the darkness at bay through dinner. As she ate dessert, she reflected that her son would arrive tomorrow afternoon. He would know what to do about the Dark Presence. In the meantime, the dog would stay in her room tonight, and she would take him with her tomorrow.

As she washed dishes, the air in the room chilled noticeably, and she heard a scratching sound at the cellar door. The dog growled, and she hastily dried the last cup and hurried to her room. The scratching sound ceased when she shut her bedroom door, and the icon glowed reassuringly on the wall.

It was easier to ignore the Dark Presence the second morning. She dressed hastily and opted to eat out rather than cook breakfast. The dog leapt eagerly into the car when she opened the door, delighted to ride with her as she did errands.

They were taking a stroll at the local park that afternoon when her son called to say he'd reached Cody. She asked him to remove the laundry from the dryer, and he agreed with a laugh. "Putting me to work already?" he teased.

"That's what moms do," she said.

The dog entered the house without hesitation that evening, barking joyfully and jumping all over her son. "I'm happy to see you too," he said, rubbing behind its ears.

She'd decided not to mention the Dark Presence. She didn't want her son to think she was crazy.

Later, over dinner, her son said, "I folded the laundry and put it on your bed. It smelled a little musty. You may want to wash it again."

"Thanks, son," she said, serving herself more pasta.

"That cellar is real creepy," her son continued. "It felt like someone was staring at me the whole time I was down there. Gave me goose bumps!" He laughed uneasily. "But that's stupid, right?"

A huge BANG from the den cut off his last word. Mother and son stared at each other, aghast. Her son leapt through the door, switching on lights as he raced toward the den. The dog stayed on his heels until they reached the den. It stopped in the doorway and growled. The mother stood behind the dog and stared at the huge encyclopedia lying on the floor. Normally, the book stood in the middle of the desk between two bookends.

"That's weird," her son said, picking up the encyclopedia and returning it to its place on the desk. "I wonder how that fell." He glanced around uneasily and then hurried her back to the kitchen, closing the den door firmly behind them.

They finished dinner in silence, and then she retreated to her room to read while her son watched TV with the dog. He stopped by her room to stay goodnight, and the dog jumped on the bed. Her son laughed incredulously. "I thought the dog wasn't allowed on the bed!"

"That was your father's rule," she said, rubbing the dog's ears fondly. She kissed her son goodnight and turned out the light.

She woke in the middle of the night, heart pounding in fear, but was unable to say why she'd awoken. The dog was growling, and the holy icon on the wall glowed brightly as it kept darkness at bay. Then she heard a terrible scream from her son's bedroom. She realized it was the second scream she'd heard. It was his first cry that had woken her. She leapt out of bed, motherly instinct overriding her fear. She grabbed the icon off the wall and charged into the hallway, just as her son bolted out of his room.

"In there! In there," he screamed, pointing toward the door. "A dark shadow, hovering at the foot of my bed!"

Chilled, she watched the bedroom door swing open. A looming shadow floated into the hallway and hovered between them and the rest of the house. She held up the glowing icon, body shaking with fear. "Leave my son alone," she shouted. The dog growled and pressed against her legs as she recited the words of the Lord's Prayer.

Slowly, the Dark Presence fell back toward the living room, forced away by the powerful icon. She pressed forward one step, then two. She could hear something scratching on the cellar door as the black shadow fled toward the den.

"Pack your bag. Right now," she told her son. She stood in the hallway dressed only in a nightgown, icon held high to ward off danger as he raced to obey her. Then he held the icon as she threw her belongings into a bag.

They fled past the scratching cellar door and burst through the front door with cries of relief. She drove them to the nearest hotel that accepted dogs and booked rooms for several days. In the morning, she called the local realtor and put her house on the market. Then her son made some calls and located a house they could rent down in Jackson. They hired a moving company to pack up the house and then left Cody, never to return.

Mother and son never spoke of the Dark Presence to each other or anyone else. But they hung the holy icon on the wall of her bedroom as soon as they moved into their new home, and purchased a second holy icon soon after for her son's room. Just in case.

PART TWO

Powers of Darkness and Light

14

Fire!

A woman I met taking photographs of the autumn sunrise over Yellowstone River told me she'd seen mountain bluebirds two days ago while driving along the East Entrance road. My eyes bulged with excitement. Bluebirds! I'd been looking for mountain bluebirds for days. And this woman had spotted them while driving along the road. It wasn't fair!

I queried her about the location of said bluebirds, and she directed me to the burnt-out section of woods beside the Nine Mile Trailhead, a few miles east of Fishing Bridge. "You know, the place where the 2003 fire burned all the trees along the road," she explained. "There's some gorgeous photography at that spot. The fall foliage is at its peak, and the wildflowers are lovely." Sounded like my kind of place! I thanked her and hurried off.

A storm rolled in as I drove along the East Entrance road. The wind was whipping across Yellowstone Lake. There were whitecaps on the water, and large waves crashed on the shore. It looked so wild and lovely that I had to stop for a moment and take pictures. I stopped again when I reached the thermal features at Steamboat Point. I snapped photos of the wind blowing steam over the lake, and then got a couple of humorous photos of two ravens that landed on the stone wall on either side of me.

"I'm looking for bluebirds, not Heckle and Jeckle," I told them, referring to two magpies in an animated cartoon I'd seen as a child. The raven on my left—feathers blowing in the wind—completely ignored me, gazing steadfastly at the rolling waves. The raven on my right sidled a step closer and blinked its eyes winsomely until I laughed aloud.

"No, I am not feeding you," I told it. It fluffed up its feathers and narrowed its eyes happily. I leaned against the stone wall, as content as my companion. The raven and I watched the storm moving over the lake as the cold autumn wind stole my breath away and the thermal features steamed gently below. When my ears went numb in the cold breeze, the ravens and I parted company, me to my car and the ravens to the picnic area below.

The parking lot to which the photographer had directed me was just ahead. I took a right turn and drove to the back of the lot, where I parked my car and got out. The woods surrounding the parking area were a mass of blackened and weather-worn gray trunks. This place was at the heart of the 2003 East Fire, and the lodgepole pines had not regrown here. Instead, grass and bushes and many flowering plants created a meadow among the dead trees. Some of the blackened trunks had fallen to the ground, forming geometric patterns among the colorful autumn leaves. I had no idea a dead forest could look so beautiful!

I passed the marker for the Nine Mile Trailhead and stood looking east into the burnt forest, marveling at an expanse of yellow grass that seemed to glow against the stark, blackened tree trunks. The land took a small dip at the far end of the parking lot, and the profusion of flowers—especially the fireweed whose leaves had turned lovely shades of red and pink and orange—drew me down the slope into the burnt woods. I clambered over a huge fallen trunk with my camera and started taking pictures of the flowers and the enticing patterns made by the broken trees. Every step seemed to reveal a new wonder to be photographed.

I barely noticed the silence that had fallen over the burnt-out grove. No bluebirds fluttered through the fire detritus. No leaves rustled. No crickets chirruped. The storm winds died away to nothing as I wandered deeper into the burnt grove. The only sounds were my footfalls and the click of the camera. I was only about ten yards from my car, but I might have been in another world, far away from the lake and its whitecaps.

Absorbed as I was in my photo shoot, something about the fire-gouged area was raising my hackles. Perhaps it was the silence? It was an eerie quiet, especially given the storm clouds overhead. What had happened to the wind? And why couldn't I hear birds singing? The only noise was the swish of my skirts and the clicking of the camera.

I was taking a picture of a flower when a man's voice spoke in my ear. I heard it clear as day. He was calling out some kind of instruction, like a man working to put out a fire. I jumped with a faint shriek and nearly dropped the camera as a second man's voice responded in kind. Then the silence returned.

I stood panting, heart beating and hands shaking. I looked all around me, but no one was there. I jumped up on a log and stared into the parking lot. It was empty.

I stood shaking like a leaf. *What in the world?* The eerie silence returned as I timidly returned to my photography. It was a listening silence. It wasn't pushing me out, but it wasn't welcoming me, either.

I took a few steps deeper into the grove, pure bravado on my part. I was terrified by the silence and by that voice in my ear. And then the world burst into flame! The log in front of me started burning, and then everything was burning—grass, trees, bushes. Hot spots torched skyward with a roar, and I could feel the heat and hear the sputter and crackle and hiss as the world around me burned.

The grove was overwhelmed with masses of gray smoke, tinged orange by the flames. It billowed up and up toward the sky and filled every inch of space between the dying trees. I tried to scream, but my cry turned into a choked gasp as smoke filled my lungs. I stumbled backward, away from the blaze, and tripped over a flaming log. I gave a muffled shout of alarm and time stretched for an eon as I fell. When my body hit the ground, the fire vanished and once again the burnt-out grove stood silent and still among the autumn flowers.

I leapt to my feet, hurdled the tree that had tripped me, and raced back toward my car. I half-fell onto the large fallen log that stood as the last barrier between me and the parking lot, and that was the moment when the wind returned. I lifted my head sharply, my hair blowing wildly around my head in the sudden cold breeze, and that's when I saw the bluebird flying over my head, heading back into the burnt grove.

I followed the bird with my gaze, feeling it was significant in some way but not understanding how. I took a seat on the large log beside the parking lot, and as soon as I sat down, several more bluebirds flew into the burnt grove. The birds darted here and there among the fallen trees, occasionally stopping to rest on broken-off branches. I could hear them chirruping merrily, but the eerie silence was still there underneath, scarcely veiled by these small signs of life. The sense of listening and watching remained.

One female bluebird caught my eye as she flew to the top of a dead stump about eight feet tall. I stared at her fixedly, as if she had a message for me. She stared back at me, uncannily still. I felt frozen in time, caught somewhere between the past and the present as the birds flittered about in the burnt grove. My whole body was covered with goose bumps.

Why am I lingering in this spooky place? I wondered.

The response came at once, as if the burnt grove whispered the answer to me: *Just be here. Witness what is happening.*

This is a haunted place, I thought, remembering my terrifying vision of the fire. *It is haunted by the fire that burned through here and the people and creatures the fire impacted.*

So I sat silently, as if under a spell, watching the birds and listening to the silence. The wind rose around me and started to howl. I heard high-pitched, anguished voices wailing in the wind, not quite human, not quite animal—or perhaps a little of both. The voices faded and then grew strong, faded and grew strong again. After ten frozen minutes, the wind abruptly died away.

On the tree stump opposite me, the female bluebird shook her feathers and flew away. In that moment, I was released from the spell that held me frozen on my log seat. I sprang up, relieved, and hurried to the car.

I hesitated with my hand on the door handle. I hated to flee like a coward. There were several beautiful autumn shots I wanted to take in this parking lot, and I still hadn't gotten a

FIRE!

picture of the bluebirds. I took a deep breath and stepped away from the car, clutching my camera tightly as I evaluated the surrounding scenery for photo opportunities.

I spent the next five minutes walking around the parking lot, taking pictures of flowers and and bluebirds and fall foliage. My nerves jangled with every click of the camera and I jumped whenever a bird called. When a passing car backfired on the road above, my nerve broke. I'd proved to my own satisfaction that I wasn't running away from this haunted place. It was now time to . . . retreat with haste!

I put the lens cap on my camera and climbed into my car. I needed a solid dose of reality after my experience in the grove. Maybe I should head up to Hayden Valley and get caught in a bison jam. You couldn't get much more real than that. Ignoring the smell of wood smoke that wafted from my dress and coat, I turned on my left blinker and drove out onto the main road. I did not look back.

15

Kahn Hayn

DRAGON'S MOUTH SPRING, MUD VOLCANO

Poor Kahn Hayn. Orphaned as a young child. Never married. No close family. It was a sad situation for a man to be in. Kahn Hayn had no one to call his own, which made him a poor man by his tribe's standards. But Kahn Hayn had a warm heart, and he was a good hunter and warrior. Kahn Hayn always looked out for those who were less fortunate, and his heart yearned for the greater good of his people.

Now, Kahn Hayn and his people lived in a troubled time. The Earthmaker had finished creating the world and had placed most of its inhabitants into special homelands perfectly suited to the tribes that lived there. But there were several tribes still wandering homeless through the Earth, and Kahn Hayn's people were among them.

One day, the Earthmaker called all the homeless tribes to a central gathering place so he might speak to them. The Earthmaker told the homeless ones that He had one final place on this great Earth that was still uninhabited. This space could become the homeland of one of the homeless tribes. However, someone from one of the tribes would have to undertake a very difficult and dangerous journey to get there.

Instantly, warriors in each of the homeless tribes volunteered to undertake the dangerous task on behalf of their people. So the Earthmaker brought the warriors, including warmhearted Kahn Hayn, to a place that was surely the desolate end of the earth. The ground was white and salted so that nothing would grow. There were no animals or trees or rivers. Everything was silent except for the wind, which blew among fantastical rock formations.

As the tribesmen moved deeper into this desolation, steam belched forth from the ground. Mud churned and popped in stinking holes in the dirt. Hot water bubbled in pools and vented forth in boiling streams.

This is a place of nightmares, thought Kahn Hayn. He jumped in shock when a great clap of thunder shook the earth underfoot. Just over the ridge, a huge cone spouted mud thirty feet into the air. Kahn Hayn clapped his hands over his sore ears to mute the terrible roar, afraid he would go deaf.

Then the Earthmaker called the warriors over to the most terrible pool of them all. It was a deep cauldron of boiling water that surged forth from the mouth of a dark cave, smashing against jagged rock walls. Steam vented from the dark interior, thundering and thumping and hissing like a dark creature trying to break free. Kahn Hayn stared into the tossing, churning water, mesmerized. Droplets from the steam soaked his hair and skin, and still he could not look away from the boiling water.

Gradually, he became aware of shouting. He looked up to see that most of the warriors had backed away from the terrible pool. Some had turned tail and were fleeing away through the boiling landscape, careful even in their fear to give the mud volcano a wide berth.

Only a handful of warriors from the various tribes remained. The Earthmaker pointed into the dreadful, boiling cauldron and said, "This land that surrounds us will belong to the tribe of any man that will dive into this pool."

"This land?" gasped the warriors. "This desolate place?"

Kahn Hayn, eyes fixed on the steaming mouth of the cave and the dreadful churning waters of the pool, listened as the tribesmen argued among themselves. This wasteland had no animals, no plants. There was nothing but mud and boiling water and steam. What kind of land was this? No one in their right mind would claim such a place. Why risk the life of a valuable warrior for a desolate land?

Kahn Hayn looked at the Earthmaker. Why had the Earthmaker, God of all he surveyed, brought them here? The Earthmaker was a good God who provided good things to the people. But he was not above testing their mettle to see what they were made of. There was more to this situation then met the eye, Kahn Hayn decided.

"I will do it," he announced loudly, cutting through the babble of words behind him. Everyone turned to look at Kahn Hayn, standing on the edge of the dreadful, boiling pit.

"No, Kahn Hayn. This is ridiculous. No one should go near that pool. Not for such a meager reward," his fellow tribesmen told him. But Kahn Hayn insisted.

"I have no family to mourn me if I die," said Kahn Hayn. "I will try this thing."

Everyone took a step back as Kahn Hayn threw down his weapons and climbed to the very mouth of the seething pit.

KAHN HAYN

Kahn Hayn looked directly into the eyes of the Earthmaker, who stood silent and still, watching him. Then he dove headlong into the boiling pool.

Burning heat engulfed him, searing every part of his body. The agony was so great that he wanted to scream, but to do so would mean death by drowning as well as burning, so he kept his mouth and eyes tightly shut. The superheated water pummeled him back and forth, up and down. The thumping and roaring sound coming from the cave reverberated through the water, shaking his blistering body. He prayed that death would come quickly and knew it must, for his body was so hot he felt numb with it, and the pain lessened a bit.

Then Kahn Hayn realized that he could not die, not until he accomplished his task. Surely there was something he must do in this pool to fulfill the expectations of the Earthmaker, some great deed that would make this agonizing death worth the pain. But Kahn Hayn did not know what he was supposed to do. The Earthmaker had not told him. Should he touch the bottom of the pool? Swim into the cave and confront the monster within? Kahn Hayn realized with despair that he could not accomplish either of those tasks. He was completely disoriented within the superheated water. Which way was up? He didn't know, and he did not dare open his eyes to check his direction, lest they burn out of their sockets.

The heat-induced numbness fogged his brain. He was boiling to death inside this pool and could struggle no longer. His skin was blistered and his nerves screamed in terrible pain. Every inch of his body that wasn't burned by the hot water was bruised by the sharp rocks covering the walls and bottom of the pool. And his air was running out. There was no hope left for Kahn Hayn, so he ceased struggling and let himself float toward whatever destiny the Earthmaker had in store for his dead spirit.

Suddenly, Kahn Hayn felt blessed cool air touch his back. Realizing he had floated to the surface of the pool, he flipped himself over with the last of his strength so he might draw in one final breath of air. And then hands were pulling him out of the water, and Kahn Hayn heard his people cheering and calling out his name.

Kahn Hayn opened his eyes and stared up into a blue sky that was fringed with leafy green trees and tall pines. This astonishing sight was soon replaced by the faces of his people, who pulled him to his feet and pounded him on his back, which—just as astonishingly—was not sore at all. Blisters, burns, and bruises were all gone, as was the desolate land through which Kahn Hayn had followed the Earthmaker on his quest. They were now surrounded by a fertile country filled with deep forests, wide meadows, flowing rivers, lovely lakes, and sparkling waterfalls. Animals of every shape and size roamed the land and inhabited the lakes and streams. Birds sang, insects buzzed, crickets chirruped. The hot springs and bubbling mud pots were still there, but now Kahn Hayn viewed them as interesting natural features that added a special touch to this landscape of abundance.

Of the Earthmaker and the rival tribesmen there was no sign. They had vanished when Kahn Hayn dove into the pool, and the rest of the tribe had miraculously been transported to this new homeland.

The tribe celebrated for many days following Kahn Hayn's triumphant return from the deadly cauldron. Prayers of thanksgiving were given to the Earthmaker. Kahn Hayn became the chief of his tribe and was given his choice of wife from among the fair maidens.

Because of Kahn Hayn's courage and the people's deep faith, the Kiowas became a preeminent tribe of this land, and they will always be held close to the heart of the Earthmaker, who is God.

16

Yancey's Ghost

ROOSEVELT

I overheard the Roosevelt wranglers talking about Yancey's ghost while I sat quietly on the benches beside the check-in booth, waiting for the one-hour horseback riding trip to begin. The other participants had not yet arrived, so the wranglers spoke freely among themselves, forgetting I was present.

"I barely got any sleep," a blonde-haired wrangler complained. "The dang ghost started banging his tin cup on the walls of the staff quarters at three a.m.!"

"I think Yancey likes you! I've never heard him so active as he was last night," a dark-haired girl teased her friend.

"Baloney!" the blonde retorted.

"Well, he certainly has never unsaddled my horse for me," the dark-haired girl said with a mischievous grin. "Wish he would, at the end of a long day! I could use the break."

"I told you, it had to be one of the guys who removed that saddle," the blonde said. "You know they like to tease me about Yancey's ghost."

"You were the only one left at the stable," the dark-haired girl said. "Everyone else had gone to dinner."

YANCEY'S GHOST

This interesting bit of ghost lore was interrupted by the arrival of a large family group, so I never did hear what other antics were being blamed upon Yancey's ghost.

As more people assembled for the one-hour ride, I mused upon what I'd heard. The ghost the girls were referencing had to belong to Uncle John Yancey, a veteran of the Confederate Army who came west after the Civil War to prospect for gold. Yancey showed up in Yellowstone in the 1870s, shortly after the park was created, and built first a mail station and then a hotel in "Yancey's Hole." The hotel provided accommodations and provisions to the stagecoach traveling back and forth between Mammoth Hot Springs and the mining camps in Cooke City. It boasted five bedrooms and could accommodate twenty guests. Rooms were two dollars per day, ten dollars per week, and included meals. There was also a saloon handy for anyone wishing a splash of moonshine after dinner. Each bedroom contained a single bedstead and a box for a bed stand on which stood a washbowl, pitcher, and towel. The partitions were made of cheesecloth, and cracks in the outer log walls were blocked up with newspaper. The "bridal suite"—Room Number One— was gussied up with a looking glass. (Oh boy!)

At this juncture in my musings, the wranglers called us together for a safety lecture, and then we were each assigned our horses. "Make careful note of your horse's name," a young man informed me as he handed me the reins of a tall chestnut. "We will be calling each person by their horse's name. This is Stubbs."

"Hello, Stubbs," I said, rubbing under the horse's chin. Stubbs leaned into my hand, enjoying the contact. The wrangler held the horse while I mounted, then left me and Stubbs to wait for the trail ride to begin. The head wrangler signaled to the group and a line of horses wound slowly out of the corral in front of me. Somehow, I'd ended up at the back, probably because I was a solo traveler. I steered Stubbs behind a fancy black-and-white paint horse and headed out on the trail.

As we traveled across the road into the sagebrush fields opposite the corral, I amused myself by imaging what it might have been like to meet Uncle John Yancey as a hotel guest, back in the 1890s. According to my reading, Yancey was a quirky old-time pioneer—perhaps the last of that breed—who was popular with just about everybody in the park and its vicinity. He had important friends among the posh families back east, some of whom dropped by the hotel from time to time. Yancey knew all the good fishing holes and had plenty of tall tales to amuse people. He welcomed all and sundry with a libation of "Kentucky tea," reputed to be the best whiskey in the park.

"Keep an eye out for badgers," one of the wranglers called, interrupting my thoughts. "They live in the holes hereabouts and sometimes peek out when they hear the horses walking by."

Obediently, I looked for badgers, and then turned my attention to the gorgeous mountain scenery and the tantalizing glimpses of the Pleasant Valley below us. As we descended slowly into Yancey's Hole, the bickering voices of two teenagers riding in front of me faded away.

And so did the hot summer day. I blinked in surprise at the suddenly colorful scene unfolding around me. The aspen trees were golden with fall leaves. The fireweed boasted a variety of colors—reds, oranges, some pinks. The riders in front of me had changed too. They were wearing rough outdoor clothing circa 1895, and the guides up front looked like real tough cowboys who'd seen some action. There were dark clouds overhead, and it began to snow as the riders wound their way through the valley toward a couple of log cabins at the far end, the larger of which was surrounded by a low fence.

As cold snow settled on my shoulders and head, I realized that the person riding two horses ahead of me wore a fancy hat and a long skirt trailed over the sides of the horse. It was a woman.

"Are you all right back there, Shirley?" a man called from farther up the line. He was more spruced-up than the others. "Would you like my coat?"

"I'm fine, Henry," the lady called back.

A man with bushy hair and a straggly beard and mustache came out of the larger of the two buildings. He buttoned his ill-fitting jacket and leaned against the fence near a grazing bay horse, watching the riders approach along the dirt road. Snowflakes landed on his hat and arms. I could see skis piled up on the side of the cabin, in preparation for the snowy weather.

The door of the saloon opened and a man reeled out. Red-faced and jolly, he looked as if he'd been drinking Kentucky tea by the bucketful. "Where's Yancey?" the man bellowed cheerfully, staggering toward the hotel. "I need another drink!"

"Disgraceful behavior," Shirley said from somewhere in front of me.

At that moment, someone bellowed in my ear: "Yo, Stubbs! Are you all right?" The world wavered and grew misty for a moment. I blinked several times, trying to clear my senses. Then I was looking into the sunlit face of a wrangler, his horse walking beside mine. "You fell behind the group," the wrangler said. "Has Stubbs been eating grass? You need to pull him up when he does that." The wrangler demonstrated the technique.

"Pull him up. Right," I mumbled. I glanced down at Stubbs, who trudged along as if nothing untoward had happened.

The wrangler motioned us ahead of him, and I urged the rambling Stubbs onward until I was once again behind the quarreling teenagers. I glanced across the valley and saw only the tree-lined hill and the little pavilions off to the left where the Roosevelt cookouts were held. No log cabins. No man leaning on the fence. No Shirley. Had I been dreaming?

The horses left the old stagecoach road, and we climbed a steep slope to the top of the ridge and then turned back toward the Roosevelt corral. My head was beginning to pound, and I still felt absurdly cold on this hot summer day. I glanced behind me into Yancey's Hole, shimmering in the summer heat. A bison wandered along the edge of the valley as the lead wrangler told us a corny joke from her place at the front of the ride. I shivered and turned away from Yancey's Hole, eager to get back to the stables and normal life.

Back in my frontier cabin, I looked up the story of John Yancey to see how it ended. John F. Yancey was seventy-seven years old when he traveled to Gardiner, Montana, to witness the dedication of the Roosevelt Arch by President Theodore Roosevelt on April 24, 1903. Yancey met President Roosevelt during the ceremony, but he caught a cold at the event and died of pneumonia a couple of weeks later.

I learned that Yancey was buried in the old Tinker's Cemetery, so when I arrived in Mammoth a few days later, I hiked up the Old Yellowstone Trail to see his tombstone. The inscription said: UNCLE JOHN F. YANCEY DIED MAY 7, 1903, AGED 77 YRS.

I remembered the man in the scraggly beard leaning against the fence. Was that Yancey? Or was it just my imagination playing tricks on me in the hot summer sun?

According to his obituary, Uncle John Yancey endeared himself to everyone with whom he came in contact—including President Teddy Roosevelt and many prominent senators and congressmen, who visited him annually in his home in Pleasant Valley. If the old frontiersman's ghost had returned to his old stomping grounds many years later to tease the local hotel staff, who could blame him? He'd lived much of his life in Yellowstone National Park, which by my reckoning was about as close to heaven as you could get on this old earth. So why shouldn't he return now and then for a visit? I would, in his place.

Happy haunting, Uncle John.

Sasquatch

LAMAR VALLEY

The Ranger grinned at Bill as they saddled their horses. He had invited his childhood best friend to take an informal day trip with him into the backcountry of Lamar Valley, sometimes called the Serengeti of North America. Bill was as excited as a little boy at the thought of riding horseback through Yellowstone.

"Maybe we'll see a grizzly bear," Bill enthused as he tightened the cinch.

"I am not sure you want to encounter a grizzly bear while riding a horse," the Ranger said dryly.

"True," Bill said, looking crestfallen. But he cheered up immediately as they mounted their horses and headed down the trail. Bill was like a little kid when it came to big animals. He still got excited whenever he was caught in a bison traffic jam, pulling out his camera to get photographs of the big bulls wandering lazily down the center of the road.

As the two friends headed along the Lamar River trail, the Ranger pointed to a grouse that flurried underneath a bush as they rode across a wide meadow filled with tall golden-brown grass, sagebrush, and few trees. Bill kept his eyes open and his mouth shut, searching avidly for wildlife as the warm sun beat

SASQUATCH

down on the two friends and summer breezes swirled across their faces, bringing the scent of sage into their nostrils.

Bill was triumphant when he was the first to spot pronghorn grazing in the valley. The Ranger didn't mention that his moment of inattention was due to the fact that he was studying the grizzly bear tracks and several-days-old scat on the trail in front of them. A bear had crossed here a couple of days ago, the Ranger decided.

The lower part of the trail was wide and meandered close to the park road. Bill saw enough bison to satisfy even his wildlife enthusiasm, and the Ranger scanned the herd with an experienced eye, noting that one of the bulls was limping. The wolves would be watching that one. Then they moved to the upper section of the trail, heading deep into the wilderness. This part of the trail was rather marshy in places, and the Ranger kept an eye on Bill, who was not a good horseman. He spotted a badger and pointed it out to his friend. Bill, who had never seen a badger before, was so excited he nearly toppled off his mount. The Ranger suppressed a grin and cheerfully held the reins so Bill could take a picture with his camera.

Bill coped quite well in the steeper sections of trail as they moved deeper into the backcountry. There was a patrol station at the far end of the trail, which stood high in the Absaroka Mountains. But the Ranger wasn't thinking about the patrol station. He was gazing down at a set of huge footprints in the trail in front of them. The prints weren't grizzly or black bear. They looked like the huge feet of a giant gorilla. (*Or a giant man*, the back of his mind whispered to him.) But that was impossible. There were no wild gorillas native to Yellowstone—

or native to anywhere in the United States, for that matter. Unless one had escaped from a zoo?

The Ranger's horse walked through the tracks as he dithered in his mind about their source, obliterating them before he could stop for a closer look. The Ranger cursed himself for his indecision and inefficiency. Now he would never know what it was he'd seen.

The men stopped for lunch up at the top of their backcountry loop, near the patrol station. Sandwiches and trail mix went well with the fresh air and lovely scenery. Bill perched on a fallen log and wolfed down his food while the Ranger kept an eye on the horses, communing together at the pine where he'd tied them.

They saw a large male elk on the afternoon leg of their journey, to Bill's great delight, and the Ranger saw more of the huge man-shaped footprints. This time, he dismounted to have a better look. He measured the bare footprint. It was twenty inches long with the toes curled under slightly and the arch pressed down into the dirt. The ball of the foot was disproportionately wide, unlike that of a human male. The Ranger slid off his own boot to check his foot. Yes, the ball of his foot was proportionate to the rest of it. But the one in this print was not.

"What are you doing?" called Bill from his horse. "Do you have a stone in your shoe?"

The Ranger shook his head and motioned for silence. He pulled out his pocket camera and took a few photos of the prints. Then he slid his boot back on and mounted again. He didn't know what had made these prints, and he wasn't sure he wanted to know. Perhaps it was a joke of some kind? (*Perhaps it was a Sasquatch*, whispered an irritating voice in his mind that refused to be silenced.)

As they continued along the trail, the Ranger tried to calculate the mass of something that had such a large and heavy footprint. Half a ton? More? He gulped.

They were still three miles from the trailhead when Bill gave an excited yip and pointed. "Grizzly bear, over by that tree. It's standing on its hind legs," he gasped, trying to keep his voice soft so he wouldn't alarm horses or bear.

The Ranger looked in the direction Bill was pointing and halted his horse, squinting in disbelief. "Bill," he said. "That's not a grizzly."

The creature was nine feet tall, covered in long, brown-black hair. It had a large, squashed-in face similar to that of a gorilla. The huge hair-covered body had a barrel chest that was at least seventy-two inches in circumference, and its arms were extraordinarily long. The creature's huge feet seemed to match the twenty-inch proportions that the Ranger had measured farther up the trail. The beast had to weigh about nine hundred pounds, the Ranger reckoned.

The wind blew the scent of musk and garbage over them. Both horses were staring over at the creature, ears pricked in curiosity. *They aren't afraid of the beast*, the Ranger noted in surprise. The creature, on the other hand, was regarding horses and riders with alarm tensing every muscle of its huge body.

"What is it, then?" whispered Bill from behind him.

"Sasquatch," the Ranger said reluctantly, just as the huge creature bolted from underneath the tree and galloped away through the golden-brown prairie grass and sagebrush. When its trajectory brought it within range, the Sasquatch grabbed a handful of pebbles and threw them at the men as if trying to discourage them from following. The Ranger kept a tight rein on his horse as pebbles cascaded to the ground several yards away. He had no intention of following the creature, which dodged behind a large sage, ducked around a tree, and then disappeared into the forest.

"Oh, my gosh," Bill gasped. "Did we just see Bigfoot? Did we?"

"Absolutely not," the Ranger said firmly, watching the swaying foliage settle into stillness as the black-brown figure vanished into the woods. "There is no such thing as Bigfoot, remember?" He turned in his saddle to look at his friend. Their eyes met, and a silent understanding passed between them.

"That was one heck of a grizzly," Bill said dryly.

The Ranger nodded in approval. "Yes, it was," he said, turning back to the trail.

They'd almost reached the trailhead when Bill said, "Is it all right if I tell my wife about the 'grizzly' we just saw?"

"Can she keep a secret?" the Ranger asked doubtfully.

"Heck yeah, she's married to me, remember?" Bill said cheerfully.

"True," said the Ranger and gave reluctant permission.

When the Ranger got home that night, he uploaded the pictures he'd taken onto his computer and gazed at the huge footprints. Sasquatch. Who would believe it? People saw the darnedest things in Yellowstone. And some of them, like today's sighting, were best left off the record.

He hit the "save as" command and put the pictures into a special folder on his hard drive called "Amazing things I've seen." This picture definitely qualified!

18

The Sentinel

DUNRAVEN PASS

I don't know why I let my friend Johnny talk me into taking an all-day Yellowstone tour. I hadn't intended to visit Yellowstone at all on this trip. But Johnny, who is Crow on his mother's side, told me he had "important business" in Yellowstone this weekend and that I should come along. And who was I to argue with a medicine man?

"But why an arranged tour? Why don't we just drive down in your truck?" I asked, confused by his desire to play the tourist. A longtime outdoorsman, Johnny already knew Yellowstone as well as anyone could.

"It is important," Johnny said somberly, his eyes fixed on something outside the kitchen window. I followed his gaze and saw two ravens perched on the fence, black feathers blowing in the breeze. Smoke from the Idaho fires swirled around them. They looked like two pieces of midnight against the ghostly gray.

We spent the night at a hotel in Gardiner and were up betimes for the tour, which left at six in the morning. We stopped at Mammoth to pick up a few more passengers, and I dashed inside the hotel to get some coffee, hoping that the caffeine would wake me up. As I walked back to the bus, a huge raven squawked indignantly at me from a nearby bench. Nearly gave me a heart attack. I didn't mention the raven when I rejoined Johnny on the bus. I figured he already knew.

We stopped at Mammoth Hot Springs to look at the terraces, and I got a few good shots on my camera. I made Johnny pose in front of the Devil's Thumb formation. (Should I have been surprised that a raven flew past just as I snapped the picture?)

Back on the bus, we meandered through the Hoodoos and paused for a moment to admire the obsidian cliff where Native Americans once made knife and spear points. Then we drove toward Gibbon Falls. The water tumbled in a foamy sheet over the irregularly shaped falls, roaring down eighty-four feet to the bottom of the canyon.

I found Johnny at the edge of the parking lot, communing with a nearby raven, who was eyeing tourists hopefully in spite of the restrictions against feeding the wildlife.

"What's with all the ravens?" I asked Johnny. Goose bumps ran down my arms as the large black bird tilted his head to look at me.

My friend shrugged, a sure sign that he was keeping something to himself. "You know what they say about ravens," he evaded my question, stepping into the waiting tour bus.

"No, I don't know what they say about ravens," I retorted, swinging myself in behind.

"Ravens?" the bus driver said, catching my comment. "Oh, they're everywhere in Yellowstone. Quite a nuisance; though personally I like them. There is a rich mythology surrounding ravens. Some native peoples call them the 'Keeper of Secrets' and the 'Bearer of Magic and Mysticism.'"

"Sounds impressive," said a red-haired woman. "I think she's talking about you, Harry," she called over her shoulder to her husband. Everyone laughed as the rest of the tour group found their seats. I glanced at Johnny, who was watching the black bird as it flapped lazily away.

"Shape-shifter," he murmured without turning his head. "Raven teaches people how to understand the language of animals and helps them as they move within different dimensional realms and different states of consciousness. A powerful totem."

Johnny sounded as if he was quoting someone. I shivered and buttoned my jacket. Shape-shifter, eh? I wondered if Johnny had come to Yellowstone to meet with Raven the Shape-shifter. Then I reconsidered. There were plenty of ravens living up at Johnny's place. No need to travel to Yellowstone to meet one.

We stopped at Fountain Paint Pots to see the four types of thermal features in the park: geysers, hot springs, mud pots, and fumaroles. Then we headed to Old Faithful for lunch. Johnny and I ate in the lodge cafeteria, and then Johnny wandered out into the geyser basin, indicating with a jerk of his head that he wished to be alone to meditate. I nodded and went to grab a seat near Old Faithful so I could watch the next eruption.

I'm not a crowd person, so I avoided the benches and sat among the trees standing between Old Faithful and the visitor center. I wasn't too surprised when a couple of ravens found my fallen log and perched at either end. "No shape-shifting," I told the birds sternly. "Absolutely no mystic journeys allowed while the geyser is going off." The birds ignored me, ruffling their feathers and crouching contently in the shade. Then the geyser started spouting hot water, and I forgot everything else.

I felt rather sleepy after lunch. We stopped on the shores of Yellowstone Lake to take pictures, and the cool breeze revived me somewhat. But I dozed all the way to Fishing Bridge. Johnny nudged me awake when we reached Hayden Valley so I could observe a large bison herd grazing in the nearby meadows. We pulled off the loop road again when we reached Canyon to admire the Upper and Lower Falls.

Then we drove slowly up the steep slopes of Mount Washburn toward Dunraven Pass, and I gazed sleepily at smoke plumes rising from one of the local fires, trying to stay awake. The bus driver related some interesting facts about the management of forest fires in Yellowstone, but I couldn't keep my mind on the lecture. Something was pulsing at my skin, like the deep steady rumbling of a conveyor belt. It felt very strange. I kept scratching my arms, trying to make the feeling go away.

I gazed over the trees and the valley, trying to ignore the prickling sensation. And then something thundered my name. "David!" it roared in a voice as large as the whole world. I jerked upright as if awakened from a deep sleep. *What was that?!?* I glanced frantically around, but everyone else in the bus was calm and a bit sleepy. Obviously, no one else had heard the voice.

Johnny gave me a funny look but said nothing. I shrugged apologetically and turned away, hands shaking. The bus was climbing toward the pass, and there was an amazing view from my window. But I found it hard to concentrate on the tour. I must have been dozing and imagined that voice, I decided. I probably shouldn't have ordered dessert with lunch.

THE SENTINEL

As we entered Dunraven Pass, a voice thundered my name: "David! David!" The whole mountain shook with the force of it. The voice had a growling noise within it, as if it belonged to a very large bear. I fell against the back of my seat, flabbergasted at the sound. The movement attracted the attention of the folks behind me. "Are you all right? You look pale as a ghost," the red-haired woman twittered, and her spouse handed me a bottle of water.

"I'm fine," I gulped, glancing at Johnny in the seat opposite me. I really needed to talk to Johnny about this strange voice. But not here in front of everyone.

"Drink some water," Johnny advised. I complied, and my nerves calmed a little. When we left Dunraven Pass, the prickling sensation on my skin disappeared and I sighed in relief.

"We sometimes see bears in the valley over there," the bus driver said, pulling to a stop at the top of a ridge. Everyone piled out of the bus, binoculars ready. We stood looking out over the long sweep of the valley, the smoke-tinged breeze buffeting us gently.

Then I saw it. A huge silverback grizzly bear loped across the meadow toward us. I tried to speak, tried to point the bear out to my fellow tourists, but I was frozen in place. Somewhere above me, a raven cawed as I watched as the bear grow larger with each step until it eclipsed the entire landscape with its colossal body. I held my breath as the bear apparition paused before me. "David," it growled. The grizzly bear was somehow more *there* than either valley or mountain, though I could see both through its shimmering body. "David," it growled again.

My mouth was so dry I couldn't speak. *Who are you?* I thought at the shining, mountain-size bear before me.

"I am the Sentinel," the grizzly bear roared. "I guard this place!"

Overwhelmed by sheer sound, I fainted.

I came to a moment later and found myself supported by Johnny. "What happened?" I gasped. He shook his head in warning as the bus driver bustled up.

"Are you all right?" she asked.

"He's a bit dizzy. Probably the altitude," Johnny said smoothly. "He needs to drink some more water."

"Should I call the medical team?" the bus driver asked.

"No, no," I said waving her away. I walked to the bus, knees shaking slightly, and Johnny kept a hand on my back as I climbed the steps. I gulped gratefully at the bottled water he thrust into my hand.

"Take deep breaths," he advised.

"What was that?" I muttered as the bus driver gathered the rest of the tour group.

"He told you. He is the Sentinel," Johnny said softly.

"You saw him too?" I asked.

"Of course," said Johnny the medicine man.

"Why did I see him?" I asked, shivering in my seat.

"Ask Raven," Johnny replied, returning to his seat across the aisle as the rest of the group crowded in.

The bus driver continued the tour, taking us for a brief look at Tower Falls before driving to Mammoth. She fussed over me when we disembarked in Gardiner, wanting to know if I still felt dizzy, if I needed to go to the hospital clinic.

"We had a great time," I interrupted, pressing a tip into her hand and following Johnny to the waiting truck. We had dinner reservations at the fancy restaurant in Chico, and Johnny didn't want to be late.

As I approached the vehicle, I realized the strange hump on the side panel of the truck bed was a perched raven. I stopped abruptly and stared at it. It stared back.

Johnny had called Raven a shape-shifter and said Raven could teach people how to *understand the language of animals.* I wondered suddenly if it was *Johnny* who had business in Yellowstone, or if it was *Johnny's business* to bring me to Yellowstone to meet with the Sentinel. And if so, what exactly did that mean?

I glanced from the raven to my dark-eyed, mysterious friend and knew what he would say. "That's between you and the Sentinel." And possibly also between me and Raven.

"No more shape-shifting," I said sternly to the bird on the truck. The raven gave a squawk and flew lazily away.

"Let's go, David. I'm hungry," said the medicine man.

As I climbed into the truck, I wondered if this was what Johnny's life was like *all the time.* I would probably never know. But he was right about one thing: It was definitely time to eat!

19

Little Joe's Grave

MAMMOTH

The veiled figure sat weeping beside the small grave in the Fort Yellowstone Army graveyard. She was stooped like an old woman, with a weathered face and graying hair. The gray hair was deceptive, for it made her look old, as did the lines of suffering on her face. But she was too agile to be old. And there was something else about the weeping figure that seemed sinister to the watching neighbor.

The neighbor shivered slightly, hugging the armful of flowers close to her chest as she observed the mournful figure. When the weeping woman rose and drifted aimlessly in the direction of the cemetery gate, the neighbor took her place in front of the small gravestone. The neighbor laid down her burden of flowers on the ground beside the carved inscription.

"Rest in peace, little Joe," she said.

Then she stood for a moment with her hand just touching the cool marble shoes on the cap of the headstone, remembering . . .

—

She had been so excited when she learned that a new family was coming to the fort. Fort Yellowstone was a small community where everyone knew everything about everyone else, so new arrivals were keenly anticipated and talked about. Word on the street was that the Trischmans had four children, some of them close in age to her own brood. This was good news, since the new family would be moving in right next door. Playmates for her active crew were always welcome. And folks said that George, the husband, was a pleasant fellow who was a first-class wheelwright and carpenter. He would be an asset to the fort.

The neighbor mentioned the anticipated new arrivals in a letter to a friend of hers who had recently moved to Billings from Fort Yellowstone. The response she received shook her deeply. Apparently, there was a story circulating in Billings that Margaret Trischman had tried to commit suicide by cutting her own throat with a large butcher knife behind the cowshed.

Mrs. Trischman afterward claimed that a strange man attacked her, but her claim was proved false, the letter from Billings continued. *She was taken to a mental hospital at Warm Springs, where the doctors have been attempting to cure her. That she will soon be living next door to you in Fort Yellowstone suggests she must be cured. But I would take care, my friend.*

The neighbor, after discussing the letter's contents with her husband, burned the missive so it would not fall into careless hands and cause talk among the residents of the fort. If the Warm Springs doctor and her husband believed Mrs. Trischman to be cured of her suicidal tendencies, then the neighbor and her husband would give her the benefit of the doubt. But the neighbor didn't want her children spending time at the Trischman place until she'd had an opportunity to size up Margie Trischman.

To that end, the neighbor stopped by with a welcoming pie on the Trischmans' first day at the fort. Mrs. Trischman thanked the neighbor graciously before introducing her husband and children. The neighbor didn't like the way Mrs. Trischman's eyes constantly shifted this way and that as they spoke. And she didn't like the way Mrs. Trischman snapped at her children, or the way the children nervously eyed their mother when they thought no one was paying attention. Only the husband seemed at ease, obviously delighted to have his family all together in their new home.

The neighbor avoided looking at the lurid neck scar that extended up past Mrs. Trischman's high collar and kept her first visit very short. Five minutes after knocking on the Trischman door, she walked back home, her body trembling visibly with relief. She was happy to be away from that house. Even without her friend's warning, the neighbor would have sensed that something was amiss in the Trischman home.

She discussed the brief visit with her husband that evening after the children had gone to bed, describing the tense atmosphere and the way Mrs. Trischman had yelled at her children. The neighbor asked her spouse whether they should prohibit their children from playing with the Trischmans. Her husband, after deliberating for a moment, decided they should not. "Ask the Trischman children to play over here," her husband said, unconsciously echoing her private musings. "That way, you can keep an eye on things."

The Trischman children were very well behaved during their first visit to the neighbor's home. Harry, Anna, Elizabeth, and little Joseph were polite and clean, and they got on well with her children. The neighbor considered the visit a success and invited

LITTLE JOE'S GRAVE

the Trischman children to come again whenever their mother could spare them at home.

The neighbor was hanging wet dishcloths on the clothesline in the yard around suppertime on Saturday when she heard desperate shouting in high-pitched children's voices. Footsteps pounded frantically toward her. A moment later, the three elder Trischman children burst into her yard, their faces white as snow, their eyes round with terror.

"Help, oh help!"

"She killed . . . she killed . . ."

"She's trying to cut our throats!"

The neighbor threw her arms around the sobbing children, her eyes darting all around the yard, seeking the source of their fear among the suddenly sinister shadows.

As the Trischman children poured out their tale, the neighbor hustled them into the safety of her house. "Run! Get your father and the authorities as fast as you can," she told her eldest son. "And take the rifle!"

As soon as her boy left, she barred the door against a possible invasion—for, according to the children's testimony, Mrs. Trischman had just murdered her youngest child with a hunting knife. And she was trying to do the same to the other three.

"She killed little Joe! She killed little Joe," sobbed the girls.

The neighbor wrapped the shivering children in warm blankets and heated milk for them to drink. While she soothed them, she heard men outside shouting frantically, and someone raced past her door on the way to the Trischman place. A second person pounded loudly on the front door, and the Trischman children screamed in fear. The neighbor calmed them and went to check through the window.

"It's your father," she told the Trischmans, and opened the door. George Trischman rushed inside and clutched his children to his chest, sobbing openly in relief to find them alive and well.

The neighbor's husband later described to her what they found when they reached the Trischman place. "Mrs. Trischman was sitting calmly in a chair with no knowledge of what she'd done," he said. "Her mind was a complete blank. Little Joe was lying on the floor in a pool of blood, his neck almost severed from his body. She'd cut his throat with a hunting knife and then tried to murder the other three."

The neighbor was so upset by this description that she ran outside to throw up in the bushes. Only yesterday, little Joseph had stopped by the house to tell her about a funny bison he'd seen rolling in the dust. Now he was dead. Murdered by his own mother. The neighbor kept vomiting until there was nothing left in her stomach. Finally, her sympathetic spouse led her indoors and got her a drink to wash the horrible taste from her mouth.

"Mrs. Trischman is confined to the guardhouse for the present," her husband said gently when she was calm again. "They are sending the US District Attorney to investigate. I believe that the judge will rule that Mrs. Trischman is insane. The West can do that to some people."

"George must be heartbroken," the neighbor murmured, remembering his glowing face on the day the family arrived in Fort Yellowstone. "He really loves her."

"Yes. But he has to care for his children now. There isn't anything else he can do for Margie," her husband concluded.

As predicted, the judge ruled that Mrs. Trischman was insane and she was placed on a train bound for Washington, DC, where she would be committed to the government hospital. But Mrs. Trischman escaped this fate by jumping from the train somewhere between Point of Rocks and Dailey's ranch in Pleasant Valley and landing in the Yellowstone River far below. George Trischman and Deputy Morrison searched for her body for many days, but it was never located. Folks in the fort assumed that the fall had killed Mrs. Trischman and that her body had been swept away by the river. But no one knew for sure.

—

The clang of the cemetery gate brought the neighbor out of her long reverie. She looked up and saw the strange woman hurrying down the road. Something about the way she walked seemed familiar. . . .

The neighbor shook her head vehemently, denying the suspicion even as it crossed her mind. The weeping woman could *not* be the missing Mrs. Trischman. Mrs. Trischman had died in the Yellowstone River a month after murdering her little boy. That was the only proper conclusion to the nightmare story. It didn't matter that her body was never found.

The neighbor looked at the small tombstone with the carved marble shoes at its cap. She hoped, wherever he was, that little Joseph was still laughing whenever a bison rolled in the dirt. She touched his carved name, then turned slowly and followed the weeping woman out of the cemetery.

20

The Miracle

September 10, 1882

My dear brother,

Thank you for your letter of September 2nd. It has been read aloud several times and shared among the entire Watson clan. The family was tickled by your description of the one-way fight between your sheepdog and the neighbor's goat. We laughed aloud when we read of the dog's inadvertent flight through the air and its subsequent landing in the briar patch. The children have been treating our nanny goat with a great deal of respect since reading of the incident.

You inquired about my recent trip down to the new Yellowstone National Park. Brother, it was an amazing journey! I saw hot pools of magnificent coloration, and travertine terraces that would take your breath away. There were bubbling mud pots that delighted my heart, so much did they remind me of the mud pies we used to make as young boys. But by far the most amazing features were the geysers. Brother, they spout water high into the air, while masses of steam boil forth with a wondrous roar.

As you know, I was traveling with three companions during my tour of the park. We spent a whole day in Mammoth Hot Springs before heading southward toward the geyser basin. We explored in the region of the Fire Hole River for a couple of days, seeing more geysers and hot pools than we could count! Brother, there were places where steam poured out of the ground with a hissing sound like that of a tea kettle on the boil. Amazing!

By this juncture, all four of us dearly desired some souvenir to take home as a memento of the marvels we'd seen. The park, of course, frowns upon the removal of specimens from the region. Nonetheless, when I spotted several colorful formations a few feet below the crater of a geyser we were exploring, I was determined to collect a few specimens for myself and my companions.

The hole beneath the crater was quite deep. I could not see more than a few feet into its dark depths. However, the colorful formations were close to the surface, and there were plenty of handholds I could use to climb down to them. I figured people would never notice the loss of a few bits from inside *the geyser, so I swung myself over the lip of the crater and commenced my downward climb. I was most careful to secure each hand before moving closer to my goal.*

When I reached a depth of twelve feet, I chipped off four colorful pieces from the inside of the geyser for souvenirs and put them into my pockets. Then I began a slow and careful ascent. My companions called cheerfully to me as I took hold of a large projection not far from the top. I leaned my whole weight upon it as I stretched for another handhold. And that's when the rock gave way and I plunged, screaming, into the dark abyss.

I don't know how long or how far I fell. It seemed like forever; each second prolonged into a lifetime of fear and chaos and longing for the family I was sure I had just lost. I could hear my companions shouting in panic far above me, their voices growing fainter as I fell. Then a new fear struck me. The water in a geyser was boiling hot. Even if I survived this long fall, I was going to burn to death as I drowned. An unhappy fate.

I splashed heavily, feet first, into warm water and sank like a stone. I descended, thrashing, for what felt like a thousand feet before my momentum slowed. I stretched out my hands and feet in the dark liquid, reaching for walls or floor, but felt nothing save water. Still, I was not dead yet. And, miracle upon miracle, the water was not boiling hot. It was the temperature of bathwater and felt quite pleasant to the skin. I might have enjoyed swimming in it had my circumstances not been so dire.

A strange feeling of peace stole over me as I kicked my way to the surface. In that moment, I knew that I was going to survive this ordeal. Somehow, God alone knows how, I was going to survive.

My head broke the surface of the water, and I gasped desperately for air. My head was hazy and throbbing, and I could hardly catch my breath. I stretched out my arms once more, and this time my right hand grasped rock. Hallelujah.

Far above me, I heard the faint voices of my companions echoing down through the darkness, frantically calling my name. But I could not answer. The fall had rattled my wits

THE MIRACLE

and shaken my voice all to pieces. All I could do was cling to my friendly rock and breathe.

Gradually, the voices of my companions faded away, and I knew they had given me up for dead. As well they should. I would have given up myself, but for the peace that bubbled up inside my soul that told me I would be saved. It made no sense at all. Still, I knew it to be true. It was as if a voice spoke this promise aloud.

Time passed slowly in the pitch blackness deep inside the crater. As coherence returned, I meditated upon my strange location. I decided that I had fallen at least fifty feet before hitting the warm water below. I felt my way around the walls of the cavern and discovered it to be about twenty-five feet in diameter. The slippery stone walls had few handholds; I would not be able to climb out, even if I was so foolhardy as to attempt such a feat in the dark.

I settled at last beside the rock that first sustained me up in this warm pool and waited in the darkness—for what, I did not know. The only thing of which I was certain in that dark abyss was the rock to which I clung. And yet, as the hours passed interminably within the devastating blackness, I felt no despair. There was a Presence by my side, clinging to me as I clung to the rock. I believe that God himself, or one of his angels, supported me in my hour of great need. (This is not something of which I have spoken to anyone else, Brother, but I know you will understand me, for you spoke of a similar Presence that sustained you during your recent illness.)

A long time later, I heard a sound like distant thunder, and the water stirred around me. At that moment, I realized that the geyser was preparing to erupt! I reached desperately out to the slippery walls, but there were not handholds firm enough to support me. The rumbling grew louder and the waters more turbid. In my panic, I began hyperventilating and thrashed about in despair. Then I felt a gentle pressure on my shoulder, as if a dear friend laid a soothing hand upon me. A thought came to me as clearly as if someone spoke aloud. The cone of the geyser was filling with water. As the water rose toward the surface, so would I! I just needed to keep myself afloat until I reached a place where I could climb out.

I calmed instantly, resolved to follow this simple plan. Keeping one hand against the wall for support, I felt the waters rise rapidly, carrying me upward with them. Unfortunately, the temperature was rising almost as rapidly as the water. What had been a pleasantly warm liquid during the long hours of waiting was now becoming uncomfortably hot. The sound of muted thunder was all around me now, making my ears tingle.

In a surprisingly short time, I could see light overhead, and then I was at the place where I had chipped out the colorful formations so many hours ago. The water was uncomfortably hot by now, and I knew if I waited for it to carry me to the top I would be badly burned. So I made one last great effort and reached for the stone above me, securing first one handhold and then another as I clambered up the cone.

Just ahead of the boiling water, I slithered over the lip of the geyser and slid face down to the base of the cone, my body completely spent. But the Presence was still there, urging me forward. The geyser is going to erupt! Get out of here. *I pushed myself onto all fours and crawled through the sintered white dirt—one yard, two yards, three. I heard the geyser erupt with a roar behind me and felt water droplets cascade across my skin as hot steam turned to rain. Then the world went black.*

I awoke around 7:00 p.m. that same evening and found myself in the care of strangers. It was just seven hours since I'd plunged into the dark waters of the geyser. It felt like seven years. The Presence that sustained me in that dark pit was no longer with me, but I believe this was because it had delivered me to safety and was no longer needed.

The strangers gave me food and drink and shelter for the night. In the morning, they helped me find my companions, who were camped near the Fire Hole River. To say that my companions were astonished to see me was an understatement. They stared in horror as I walked into camp, pale of face and wide of eye. At first they believed me a ghost, like Marley in A Christmas Carol. *It wasn't until I shook each of them by the hand several times that they were convinced that I was well and truly alive. Remembering suddenly the reason I first descended into the geyser, I felt in the pockets of my trousers. To my amazement, I found that the colorful formations I'd chipped out of the geyser—was it only yesterday?—were still within. I solemnly handed the colorful rocks to my companions as if handing out first prizes at the fair. And, truly, these prizes were hard-won indeed; at least by me!*

There is very little more to my story. We left for Bozeman in the morning, and from there we returned to our separate homes. The local newspaper wrote up my unbelievable story, and they did a fine job reporting the facts. I have enclosed a clipping with this letter for the edification of the family. To you alone do I entrust the entirety of the tale, and ask that this letter remain private between us.

I remain your loving brother,
Walter

The Death Pit

TOWER JUNCTION

It was a fair day in the summer of 1939 when they loaded up the car to drive out to the work site. The mountains still had snow on their peaks, but the valleys were bursting with flowers after the spring melt. The air through the windows smelled of fresh grass and sagebrush. Johnson inhaled deeply as the other members of his work crew chatted cheerfully with the supervisor.

There were three lads assigned to the crew at the proposed bridge site just east of Tower Junction: Bill Nelson, Vaughn Roley, and himself. He was the youngest of the three, just turned eighteen, but Nelson was the newest employee, having joined the staff thirteen days ago. The men worked for the Bureau of Public Roads, and today's assignment was fairly simple. The BPR regularly gathered information on the ground formation at a new work site before embarking on a project. To this end, a twenty-six-foot shaft had been sunk at the proposed bridge site, and the men were to continue working on the shaft during their shift.

When their supervisor dropped them off at the site at 8:30 a.m., Johnson took a quick, appreciative look at the flowing river below them, at the snow-capped mountains, and the meadow flowers beginning to bloom. A bison grazed in the distance, ignoring the humans on its turf.

"Stop daydreaming, Johnson," Nelson called cheerfully. "It's time to get to work!"

Roley would take the first turn at the bottom of the shaft, which measured five feet by six feet at the bottom. Johnson grinned at Roley as his colleague placed his feet into the bucket that was used to lift and lower men in the narrow space. Grabbing the handles of the hoist, Nelson and Johnson slowly lowered Roley into the pit. Johnson saw Roley gasp and sway a bit around the twenty-foot mark and wondered what was wrong with his friend. Roley quickly recovered himself, and he seemed fine when he reached the bottom of the shaft. As Johnson turned away from the hoist, Roley gave a sudden shout: "Bad air! Johnson, Nelson, pull me up!" He stepped back into the bucket and gestured for them to raise it.

Johnson and Nelson whirled back to the hoist. As they turned the handles, Roley swayed dizzily and fainted, falling out of the bucket.

"Roley!" Johnson screamed, leaning over the pit in consternation.

"I'll go down," Nelson said, catching hold of the rope.

Nelson swung himself into the shaft and slid down the rope while Johnson watched apprehensively from the top. Suddenly, Nelson's grip loosened and he dropped from the rope, falling precipitously into the pit. He landed in a corner not far from Roley's prone body. Nelson must have been overcome by the bad air, Johnson realized, his heart pounding with panic. Now there were two men in the pit breathing who knew what kind of bad fumes. And only one of him left to rescue them both.

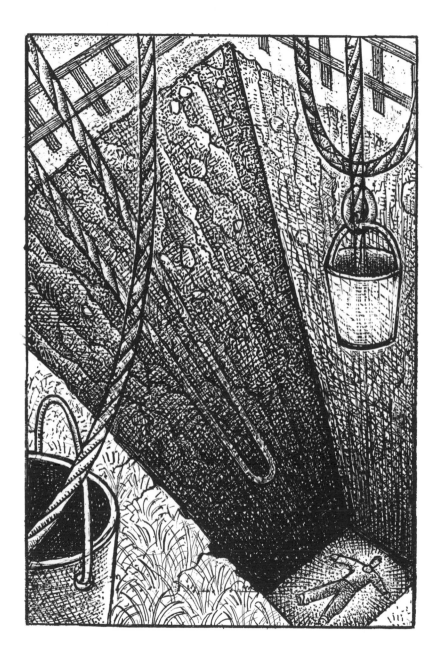

THE DEATH PIT

Johnson leaned over the pit, wondering if he should climb down himself. Then he reconsidered. If Nelson and Roley couldn't breathe down there, how could he? And if he was overcome himself, there would be no one to rescue his friends. They could all die! What should he do? Time was ticking away, and every second the workers below were breathing in toxic fumes.

Johnson's panicked eyes fell on the bucket lying in a beam of sunlight deep in the pit. Roley's feet were still trapped inside. Maybe, just maybe, Johnson could pull him out of there. *Please, God!*

Grabbing the hoist handle, Johnson began hauling on the rope. Slowly, the bucket rose into the air—five inches, then ten. Roley slowly rose with the bucket, his body flopping this way and that. Johnson prayed as he had never prayed before while the bucket bumped its way to the surface. His sweating hands slipped all over the handle as Johnson carefully hoisted his friend upward. "Please God, don't let him fall," he prayed. When the bucket drew near the top, Johnson lunged forward and grabbed Roley, hauling him out of the pit with a strength he did not know he possessed. Stinking yellow foam boiled out of Roley's nose and mouth as Johnson dragged him through loose dirt and stones and laid in him in the shade of a nearby sage.

"Wake up, Roley! Wake up," Johnson gasped, shaking his friend. "Breathe! The air is clean here. Breathe!"

After a few heart-stopping seconds, Roley took a huge breath of fresh air, and then another. Johnson hovered over Roley until his friend was breathing normally. Then he ran back to the pit to check on Nelson.

Nelson was huddled on his stomach in the far corner of the pit. Johnson could hear his ragged, unsteady breathing. Remembering the yellow foam leaking out of Roley's nose and mouth, Johnson feared that every breath Nelson took might be killing him. He had to go for help. Johnson ran back to Roley, who sat up groggily.

"Nelson is still down in the shaft," Johnson said urgently. "I have to go for help. Keep an eye on him until I get back with the ranger!"

Roley nodded weakly, and Johnson sprinted toward the Tower Ranger Station. *Hurry, hurry!* His heart pounded the frantic message as Johnson ran faster than he'd ever run before, sprinting through rocks and sagebrush until he came in view of the ranger station. He started shouting as soon as he entered the driveway, and the ranger flew out the door to meet him.

"Accident! Bad fumes in pit. Man trapped at bottom," he gasped, bending double from a stitch in his side.

Johnson bounced impatiently on his toes while the ranger called for backup, mentally urging the men to hurry. The ranger grabbed some ropes, and they rushed out to the car as several men arrived to assist with the rescue.

When they reached the work site, the rescue party found Roley swaying beside the pit with the hoist rope in his hands. He was trying without success to lasso the rope around Nelson's foot or arm so he could pull his colleague to the surface. Taking the hoist rope from Roley, the ranger tied it around the chest of a man called Brutus. Then the ranger gave Brutus a second rope to tie around Nelson's body so the rescuers could haul the stricken worker to the surface.

As Brutus descended into the dim shaft, he was overwhelmed by the smell of sulfur. Fumes filled his nose and mouth and he slumped against the rope, immediately losing consciousness. Alarmed, the men pulled Brutus back to the surface.

"I'm going down there," Roley said as they carried the unconscious man a safe distance from the pit. He grabbed the hoist rope and tied it around his chest.

"You can't, Roley. The fumes are too bad," Johnson protested. "You passed out the last time you went down there!"

"I'll hold my breath on the way down. That should give me enough time to get the loop around Nelson," Roley said. "Hurry! Nelson's still breathing in those noxious fumes!"

Taking a deep gulp of fresh air, Roley held his breath as the men lowered him into the pit. He ran out of air just as he reached the bottom of the pit and gasped desperately for breath. Noxious fumes filled his lungs, and Roley swayed dizzily. "Come on, Roley," Johnson urged as his friend staggered forward, fighting to stay conscious. With visible effort, Roley forced trembling hands toward the prone worker and slipped the rope around Nelson's foot. Then he passed out beside the stricken man.

"Haul them out," shouted the ranger.

A few tense moments later, Roley's body was eased over the lip of the pit, followed by Nelson. Stinking yellow foam fountained out of Nelson's nose and mouth as the rescuers laid him in the shade. Nelson had been in the pit around twenty minutes, by Johnson's reckoning, and was in bad shape. Roley, not feeling well himself, was also dribbling yellow foam from mouth and nose.

The ranger began first aid immediately, and the two men were rushed to the hospital over in Mammoth. Roley survived the terrible ordeal, but Nelson died the next day. It was later determined that the death pit was filled with toxic amounts of hydrogen sulfide and carbon dioxide. The experts decided it was the lethal dose of hydrogen sulfide gas that killed Nelson.

A new study of the noxious gases that sometimes leaked into the pits and caves around Mammoth and northern Yellowstone was commissioned following the deadly incident. Mammoth's Devil's Kitchen and other caves were found to contain dangerous levels of carbon dioxide and were immediately closed to tourism. They remain closed to this day.

22

Swept Over

CANYON

It was late afternoon when I left the parking lot on the north rim of the canyon to follow the hike to the brink of the Lower Falls. As I walked down the well-kept dirt trail, which descended the cliff face in a series of switchbacks, I nodded and smiled at hikers puffing breathlessly past me on their way to the top. The sunlight was filtering fitfully through the lodgepole pines, and I paused for a moment to take a photo of the Upper Falls through a gap in the trees. I had the rest of the afternoon to make the one-mile round-trip journey to the brink and back, so I didn't hurry.

"How was the falls?" I asked a stout man who paused beside me to wipe the sweat from his brow.

"Lovely! Lovely," he burbled. "Worth the hike, even the upward bit!" He flashed me a smile and continued upward, breathing like a steam engine. I suppressed a grin, realizing that I would probably sound the same in a few minutes, when it was my turn to go back up the mountain.

It took longer than I expected to hike down to the brink. I heard the roar of the Lower Falls long before I caught sight of it. I peered upstream along the curve in the river, trying to get another look at the Upper Falls, but the topography of the river obscured it from this vantage point.

When I finally twisted through the last of the switchbacks, I saw two platforms overlooking the roaring Lower Falls—an upper and a lower viewpoint. Both were empty at the moment. I had the place to myself. I was pleased, preferring solitude to the crowded conditions I'd experienced at Old Faithful and other popular places in the park.

I walked onto the lower platform, and my eyes widened as I took in the magnificent sight. The Yellowstone River seemed almost calm at the lip of the falls, churning gently as golden sunlight glinted on the dark water. Then it roared over the edge, soaring in a thunderous white spray 308 feet to the rocks at the bottom, forever hidden by the endless, rising mist.

The river rushed onward through the vast, colorful canyon beyond the Lower Falls. The Grand Canyon of the Yellowstone was all roughly hewn golden rock that smoothed unexpectedly in places into steep inclines that looked rather like a giant's sliding board. Bands of pink and red and orange streaked the walls of the canyon, creating a scene of improbable beauty. No wonder the government had sent an artist along to paint this place. No one would believe in the existence of such an amazing place without proof.

Shadows were gathering on the sides of the canyon as I leaned on the railing, staring hypnotized into the ever changing water as it flowed swiftly past me and over the edge. I was puzzled by the reddish tinge I sometimes glimpsed in the water. I heard a steady thumping noise, almost as if the water was pounding on a drum. The wind whispered around me like many voices chanting a song I almost understood.

SWEPT OVER

I shook myself from my meditations and walked to the upper platform to get a different view of the falls. To my surprise, I saw an elderly Native American gentleman dressed in a faded buckskin jacket seated on a bench in the shade of the rock face. I hadn't heard the man arrive, nor glimpsed him behind me on the trail. Still, that was hardly unusual. It was hard to hear anything above the steady pounding of the waterfall. I nodded courteously to the old gentleman and went to the upper railing to gaze into the mist filling the base of the falls. The red tinge was back among the white foam, coloring the water closest to my vantage point. It seemed rather strange.

Suddenly, the old Native American gentleman was beside me, leaning on the railing and gazing at the Lower Falls. His sudden appearance was almost uncanny. My skin prickled for a moment and I felt cold where mist droplets touched me.

"It is a beautiful sight," the old man said. I nodded without speaking. My heart was still pounding from his surprise appearance. "And a sad one."

"A sad one?" I squeaked; my voice still tight with surprise.

"On evenings like this, when the water drums beat strongly and the falls are tinged with red, I remember the old legend about this place and it makes me sad," the old man replied. "Some say that the legend is not true. Myself, I like to keep an open mind. Folklore books claim it is a tale of the Crow people, but newspaper accounts from 1870 identified the people involved in the tragedy as 'Sheep Eaters.' After all this time, who can really be sure?"

"So what is this legend?" I asked, relaxing slightly and leaning once again on the railing.

"The story begins with a group of five militiamen and their Crow guide who decided to explore the little known Canyon of the Yellowstone in April of 1870," the old gentleman began. And he told the following tale:

The white men penetrated deep into the canyon region, keeping an eye out for signs of gold while they explored. On the morning of April 2, they paused in the foothills to sink a hole into a likely spot, having seen promising signs of ore. Suddenly, their Crow guide approached the company with urgent news: A small band of Indians was camped four miles upstream. The news did not distress the explorers unduly. They had plenty of advanced weaponry among them, enough to take on a small native band if it decided to attack.

The day progressed without incident, but in the nighttime, the Indians ran off with the explorers' pack horses. When the theft was discovered at daylight, the white men pursued the thieves into the precipitous mountains. The tribesmen had a four-hour head start on the explorers, but the white men were fewer in number and gained rapidly on their quarry.

After three hours of hard riding, the explorers came suddenly upon the tribe. They were crossing the river just above the Lower Falls aboard a hastily constructed raft of driftwood held together with thongs made of buckskin and buffalo robes. A circle of men sat with their weapons at the center of the unwieldy raft while the women paddled desperately for the opposite shore with wide pieces of bark. The stolen pack horses were swimming beside the raft, which was swept precariously downstream in spite of the rowers' best efforts.

The watching explorers realized that the river current was too strong for the unwieldy craft. The paddlers were fighting a losing battle to reach the opposite bank. The horses had a better chance of success. Four of them were already climbing the bank on the far shore. Beside the explorers, the Crow guide calmly raised his rifle and fired at the retreating band. One of the braves gave a yell of pain, and an explorer cried, "For God's sake, boys, don't murder them—they are bound to go over the falls!"

At that moment, the raft was caught in an eddy and sank an inch or two below the surface so that the men and women aboard her appeared to be sitting on top of the river like water spirits or the ancient gods. It was an eerie sight. The spell was broken when a brave fired an arrow through the arm of the Crow guide. With an angry yelp, the Crow guide fired again into their midst, wounding a second warrior. The explorers had to tie up their guide to prevent him from shooting more members of the doomed band.

The raft was mid-channel now, flowing in swift water between jagged rocks. No retreat was possible, for there was no place to land. An old warrior rose to his feet, spoke a few words to the braves, and then turned his face up to the sun gleaming high above the canyon. Then he pulled his buffalo robe tightly around him and sat down again in the circle. The women wailed and clutched the edges of the submerged raft, tearing their hair in grief. But the warriors shook hands with one another and began chanting a soft death song.

The raft moved swiftly toward the edge, carrying the wailing women and the unmoving braves. The warriors gazed calmly toward the lip of the falls, where the water disappeared so abruptly with a roar like thunder. Their courage in the face of sure death silenced the watching explorers. One by one, the white men raised their hats in salute to the brave warriors below.

The white explorers would have gladly faced their enemies in battle and killed them without a qualm. But the moment when the raft, still intact, sailed out over the lip of the falls and disappeared into the roaring white foam with its human cargo was impressed forever upon the souls of the watching explorers. Stunned pity and deep sorrow shook each man to the core.

In that heart-wrenching moment, two large eagles flew over the roaring mouth of the precipice, screaming their defiance as the water thundered like drums on the jagged rocks far below. It was a fitting tribute to the bravery of the dead tribesmen below. With many backward glances, the white explorers turned their horses away from the river and rode away.

The old man paused his story as I swallowed several times and wiped my streaming eyes. He dug into his pocket and handed me a well-worn buckskin handkerchief. I dabbed futilely at my eyes, leaving mascara all over the handkerchief.

"Keep it," he said kindly.

I gave him a watery smile as he continued, "They say that the voices of the chanting warriors can still be heard at the Lower Falls, for those who choose to listen. And the water sometimes flows with a red tinge, like that of blood."

"Oh, how sad," I cried, dabbing at my eyes once more. My nose was running so badly that I had to turn away to blow it. When I turned back, the old man had vanished.

Heart thumping wildly, I hurried to the rail and looked down at the lower platform. No one was there. I hurried to the first switchback and gazed upward, but saw no one. Shivers ran up and down my spine as I sank onto the bench, rubbing my goose-fleshed arms. Where had the old man gone? I'd only turned away for a moment. *Hadn't I?*

My eye was caught suddenly by a weather-worn dead tree beside the trail. The stump was about eight feet tall, and the curve of the wood rather suggested an old man's wrinkled face. The dead tree ended in a point that might have been an eagle feather sticking up from a warrior's headdress.

Don't be ridiculous, I thought. My legs trembled as I stood up and turned my face resolutely toward the top of the canyon. It was getting late, and I had half a mile of switchbacks to follow up the rock face of the cliff. It was time to go.

As I passed the log warrior beside the path, I gave it a solemn nod. Perhaps it was the guardian of the Lower Falls. Or perhaps I was still mesmerized by the falling water and had dreamed the whole thing.

When I reached the car, I remembered the old man's handkerchief. That had been real, hadn't it? I groped around my person and my hand closed over something soft in my pocket. Icy chills ran through my body as I drew out a worn piece of buckskin streaked with mascara.

23

The Hero of Stone Mountain

STONE MOUNTAIN

Wilhelm wasn't thinking about the cold weather as he saddled up his employer's red mule on the morning of Christmas Eve 1879, though he should have been. Winter had come early in the territory and was causing great hardship among the settlers. A shortage of food had driven the wolves and coyotes down from the hills, and the starving beasts were joining together in larger and larger packs to attack anything that moved.

As the winter grew steadily worse, the ranchers sent their cattle herds to more seasonable locations, which left the hungry wolf pack fewer animals to hunt. That's when the wolves started attacking people. A peddler was dragged from his cart and devoured along with his horse. And the pack had eaten a drunken cowboy that fell off his horse. The intoxicated cowboy managed to kill six wolves before sheer numbers had overwhelmed him.

By December, there were nearly a hundred starving animals roaming the prairie in a massive pack. People were forced to defend their horses and stock against regular onslaughts. Several posses of cattlemen attempted to wipe out the giant pack with no success. The wolves had a range of a hundred miles, and the pack would fade into the hills whenever it sensed danger.

None of these facts were at the forefront of Wilhelm's mind at the moment. Dressed in a magnificent suit of cream-colored pants, white vest, and a sky-blue necktie, Wilhelm was setting forth for his wedding in Stone Mountain. The ceremony would take place at his betrothed's home, which was a good twenty-five miles from his current location. Wilhelm mounted his red mule, careful not to disturb his sartorial elegance, and set off, visions of his beautiful wife-to-be, the plump and fair Georgiana, driving every other consideration from his mind.

Georgiana was the eldest of ten daughters, born to the local brewer and his wife. The brewer had come to the territories with nothing and had built up a very wealthy business over time. Wilhelm, a waiter at a local restaurant, was astonished when Georgiana chose his suit above the rest. At first the brewer, now a very prominent citizen in the territory, frowned upon his daughter's choice. Then his wife reminded the brewer that they had *nine more daughters* to marry off. After that, the brewer welcomed Wilhelm with open arms, and the brewer also threw open his money coffers in preparation for the nuptials. There would be a merry feast following the ceremony, and the celebrating would extend throughout the winter holiday. Wilhelm could almost taste the wedding ale as his mule jogged across the icy landscape.

It was an eerie winter day. Huge cloud shadows moved randomly over the stark winter landscape, and wind devils circled across the thick snow crust. Wilhelm's dark winter coat and white wedding ensemble fit right in with the monochromatic scene. The only bright colors on the prairie were the reddish coat of the mule and Wilhelm's sky-blue necktie.

Wilhelm's mule puffed onto the mountain road after a ten-mile jog through ice and snow. They were traveling apace along the narrow road when the mass wolf pack erupted from a gorge about a mile away and swept across the prairie like a gray flood.

The wolves picked up Wilhelm's scent at once, and the ear-splitting howl that arose from the pack lifted him several inches out of his saddle and made the blood freeze in his veins. As the pack zeroed in on them, the red mule levitated off the ground and galloped in the direction of the still-distant brewer's home faster than the speediest racehorse. The rawboned creature was all ears and tail, but for the next five side-splitting miles it outran the mass wolf pack. Cold sweat poured down Wilhelm's panicked face as he struggled to stay on.

As its strength ebbed, the red mule slowed and the yelping pack drew closer to its quarry. Wilhelm's straining eyes searched for a place of refuge among the desolate canyons. The howling wolves were less than half a mile distant now. Chills raced up Wilhelm's spine as he envisioned the pack ripping him to pieces.

At that moment, the red mule stumbled at the head of a ravine and Wilhelm flew off its back and plunged to the bottom. The mule, freed of its burden, picked up speed and raced mightily toward the brewer's home. When it entered the yard with its empty saddle, Georgiana screamed, *"Mein Gott!"* and fainted while tumult and chaos prevailed among the assembled wedding guests.

Wilhelm, meantime, lay stunned at the bottom of the ravine. Heart-pounding terror forced him onto his feet, and he raced up the side of the ravine, searching for a tree to climb among the sparse shrubbery. Wilhelm could hear the pack howling as it sped closer. Alone on foot, he didn't have a chance. Then Wilhelm saw a cave in the side of the ravine. He plunged within and found himself in total darkness. Wilhelm wavered uncertainly, wondering if it was more dangerous to linger in the entrance and face the wolf pack or to wander blindly into the cavern and break his neck in a dark pit. He smiled grimly, realizing he was truly between the devil and the deep blue sea. He was empty-handed save for a flint and a small pocketknife, so no help there.

At that moment, the mass wolf pack reached the ravine. Wilhelm drew his knife and faced the entrance to the cave, determined to fight bravely to the end. To his astonishment, the main body of the pack boiled past on the trail of the red mule. Only a few stragglers broke away to nose the man-shaped indent in the snow. Still, even a few starving wolves could kill. Wilhelm hoped that the looming darkness of the cavern would give them pause. Hadn't he read somewhere that wolves didn't like caves?

A moment more brought the wolves to the entrance. The beasts, four in number, growled uneasily, glaring into the darkness and dancing anxiously outside the cavern mouth, afraid to enter the dark hole. They darted forward and back, each time moving a little closer to the cave. The famished wolves would not stay outside for long, Wilhelm realized—not with a ready meal just inside the cave.

He heard a frustrated howl rise from the mass pack up the road. They'd lost the trail of the red mule. Wilhelm heard them retracing their path, heading straight for the ravine. Desperately, Wilhelm set fire to some brush he found near the entrance. He fanned the flames as the mass pack yowled down into the ravine. The wolves halted a few feet from the flames, scrambling over one another in baffled fury as more and more animals flooded into the narrow space. Through the flickering flames, Wilhelm saw roughly sixty or seventy gray wolves, some white, and a few sneaking coyotes. The milling beasts were so thin that their ribs protruded, and their fierce eyes were ravenous with hunger. The fire wouldn't hold them for long. Muttering prayers under his breath, Wilhelm grabbed a torch from among the sparse branches and hurried into the dark depths.

Wilhelm followed an irregular passage that dwindled in size the deeper he ventured into the cavern. He was forced to bend his head to keep from bumping it, and then had to get down on his knees and crawl. The torch bounced a few times on the cavern floor as he crept forward and extinguished, leaving him in darkness so black that his torch-dazzled eyes populated it with temporary stars.

With no light and hungry wolves not far behind, Wilhelm knew he was a dead man. Commending his soul to God, he slithered onward, sometimes on hands and knees, sometimes on his belly. Suddenly, the cave expanded before him. He felt air over his head and stumbled to his feet; reaching blindly for walls or a roof to guide his faltering steps. The yelp of a wolf less than four feet behind him sent him leaping forward in a panic. He found himself on the edge of a steep incline that was slick with ice. Wilhelm's foot slipped and he plunged downward, sliding on his back for twenty yards before a rock outcropping caught his coat and jerked him to a halt.

A wolf slid past him, yowling like a lost soul. Wilhelm heard others yipping in the small cavern above. He knew that the next wolf past would shake him loose from the outcropping, so he felt along the wall until his fingers found a wide shelf just over his head. Panic drove him upward just as a second wolf came

THE HERO OF STONE MOUNTAIN

shooting down the incline, followed by a third and fourth. From his perch, Wilhelm realized suddenly that he could see the wolves hurtling down the incline. A dim light poured into the cavern from somewhere at the bottom. Following the light to its source, Wilhelm saw that the incline ended abruptly at the edge of a large pit with a narrow opening at the far side. Daylight filtered through the gap, illuminating the dark cave.

Yelping and howling in angry frustration, wolf after wolf came shooting past Wilhelm and down the steep passage. The wolves and coyotes at the front of the pack were being launched willy-nilly onto the slide by the wolves still struggling through the crawl space. Some of the wolves slid on their backs, some on their haunches, and some thrashed frantically to and fro, bodies knotted like pretzels. The look of chagrin and snarling fury on their faces as they whipped helplessly past made Wilhelm chuckle in spite of his hair-raising circumstances.

More than a dozen infuriated canines had plunged down the slippery incline when a hideous howling burst forth from the pit below. Wilhelm's head whipped around in panic, and he saw two enormous grizzly bears rise up from the bottom of the pit. The sliding wolves had fallen on top of the hibernating grizzlies, and the bears didn't like it one bit. The bruins rose on their hind legs with a roar that shook the cavern and ferociously attacked the intruders. The pit was full of whirling, biting canines as the giant bears crushed and disemboweled their foes.

Wilhelm sat with open mouth and distended eyes as he gazed upon this fight of all fights. More and more wolves plummeted into the pit as the bears bit and roared and pummeled and squeezed. Within minutes, the floor of the hole was littered with dead wolves. The survivors whined and rushed about, trying to find a way out, but the exit was blocked by the furious body of a grizzly. The bears were doing their darnedest to rid the territory of the mass wolf pack, and they seemed to be succeeding.

Wilhelm realized suddenly that all the wolves and coyotes in the mass pack had slid past him into the pit. Casting one last incredulous look down into the body-strewn pit, Wilhelm crawled along the shelf and carefully climbed to the top of the slide, using handholds on the wall to keep himself from slipping. The last thing he needed was to land on top of an angry grizzly bear.

He struggled through the crawl space and followed the dim light until he reached the entrance of the cave. Wilhelm climbed up to the road and set off on foot toward Stone Mountain. He was a little worse for wear, and his spiffy white suit was ruined, but what a story he had to tell. And tonight he would be married. *Danke Gott.*

Wilhelm was met by a frantic search party headed by his future father-in-law. Upon hearing his story, the brewer embraced Wilhelm and declared to one and all that his future son was a great warrior. The company reached Stone Mountain at dusk and Wilhelm—after taking a moment to wash and change—was married to Georgiana before God and all those witnesses. The celebration following the nuptials was merry indeed. Wilhelm was a hero as well as a bridegroom. The brass band played martial airs in his honor, and Georgiana slipped her hero a sweet kiss from time to time, to the happy roars of the increasingly intoxicated crowd.

On Christmas Day, a posse of hunters and cattlemen rode to the entrance of the cave where the wolves had fought with the grizzly bears. The large pit was filled to the rim with the gory remains of wolves, and only one grizzly bear yet lived.

It was so crippled and blind that they shot it at once to put it out of its misery. The two dead grizzly bears were of unusual size, and their fight with the mass wolf pack became an oft-told tale among the settlers in the territory. As for Wilhelm and Georgiana, they lived long and happy lives with many children and much prosperity. To his dying day, Wilhelm was known throughout the territory as the Hero of Stone Mountain.

24

Not Far Below

WEST THUMB

The campfire crackled cheerfully as I stirred the beans in the cook pot. The smell filled the little clearing by the hot springs, bringing Pa out of his tent on hands and knees, sniffing the air like a hungry grizzly bear. I grinned at his antics. "Supper in ten minutes," I told him. He grinned back at me and walked into the pines to gather more firewood from the abundant deadfall around us.

Our camp was pitched on the southwest slopes of Yellowstone Lake. Way back when, Pa had worked as a fur trader with the Rocky Mountain Fur Company and he'd first traveled through this strange land in the 1830s. Pa had been a fresh-faced boy back in those days. He was a grizzled backwoodsman now, but there was still a look of keen eagerness in his dim blue eyes as he piled wood near the fire and accepted a plate of salt pork and beans for his dinner.

Pa'd finally settled down in Fort Bridger and got himself a nice bride from among the local settlers. He raised me and my brother on stories about his adventures in the wildlands. Our favorites by far had been the stories of the strange country at the headwaters of the Yellowstone River, where geysers spouted high into the sky, mud bubbled in colorful pots, and where you could cook your dinner in boiling springs that came in colorful hues of red and yellow and orange and even green! Ma always said that Pa must have been hit on the head by a falling tree branch to tell such tales, but it turned out that everything he said was true.

There was just Pa and me now. Ma and my little brother died of fever a few years back just after I was fifteen. Pa and I'd started roaming after that, trapping and guiding folks through the area. I could hunt and fish and trap as good as Pa, and he'd taught me to carve animal figures from wood.

"Something smells mighty good," a voice hailed us from lake's edge. We turned to see a rugged, whip-thin old trapper standing with a fresh-killed partridge in one hand, a gun across his shoulder, and a quizzical smile on his face. Pa jumped up with a smile to welcome the third member of our party. The men shook hands and pounded one another on the back.

"It's about time you got back. We nearly gave you up for lost. Sit, eat," Pa said, dragging the fellow over and gesturing him to a seat on a fallen log. "Thomas has been cooking some fancy swill for dinner. Never expected restaurant fare here in the wildlands!"

The three of us laughed and set to eating with a will. Hunting and trapping honed the appetite. As the air grew cooler, the steam from the hot springs grew thick and blew across our faces, smelling of sulfur. The moist air felt good on my skin. It was my first time in Yellowstone. We'd come up the Snake River and had spent the last two nights on a small lake with hot springs. I'd seen my very first geyser, and I crowed like a young 'un at the sight. My companions had laughed at my exclamations of glee.

"It's sure something to see, ain't it?" the old trapper said kindly when the display was over for the evening. "I never grow tired of it."

I washed our dishes in the lake, watching the colors of the setting sun sparkle on the wavelets washing the shore. When I got back to the fire, the old trapper was leaning with his back against the log and his boots toward the fire, sipping coffee and gazing up at the first stars twinkling above the mountains.

"How about a story?" Pa asked, glancing toward me with a smile. I grinned back. I knew they both thought me a fresh-faced boy to be treated like a man and indulged like a child. I didn't care.

The old trapper smiled and said: "Have I ever told you about the diamond mountain of the Yellowstone? It's invisible, so you can't see it even when you're looking right at it. I only found the dang thing when I bumped my nose on a ledge while tracking deer across a meadow. Took me half a day to ride around the mountain, and I never did catch them deer. That there diamond mountain, it acts like some kind of giant telescope, don't you know. Once I looked through it and saw a dozen Crow Indians hunting elk more'n twenty-five miles away! I knocked a chunk off the mountain so I could show it to one of them scientist fellows, and he told me the invisible mountain was made of diamond."

I laughed delightedly as Pa explained that the mountain was really made of black glass, called obsidian, and that the natives used it to make stone knives and arrow points that they traded with the other tribes in the region.

"There's a little lake up that way where the beaver are near impossible to kill because of their superior cuteness," the old trapper said with a grin. "They got haunts and houses in grottoes all around the base of that diamond mountain."

"Tell Thomas about the petrified forest," Pa urged.

The old trapper complied. "Yonder over the mountains to the north and east of us is a petrified forest," he began. "A large tract of sagebrush is perfectly petrified underneath some tall stone trees. You can see every leaf and branch on the bushes, and stone rabbits, sage hens, and other animals are frozen here and there. Once I found me a petrified songbird with a petrified tune coming out of its mouth!"

I leaned against the log opposite the old trapper, whittling a piece of wood into the shape of a cougar. I gave the trapper a huge smile to egg him on.

"Tomorrow, I'm gonna take you to see a lake where the water flows toward the Atlantic and the Pacific Oceans at the same time," the old trapper said. "Then we'll head west to a place where there's so many geysers you can set yourself on a log in the center of the basin and see something going off no matter which way you spin. Some of them geysers spout more'n seventy feet straight up with a powerful loud hissing. There's a boiling pool over there that's big as a lake, with bright colors that swirl off the edges like orange and red petals."

"The river up that way is hot at the bottom," Pa put in, puffing lazily on his pipe. "When you wade through the water, you can feel warmth coming right through your boots! And there are places not far from there where steam roars out of holes in the ground like the breath of a fierce dragon."

"The Yellowstone River issues from this lake up north a piece. It flows through a twenty-mile perpendicular canyon where mighty waterfalls roar and foam over tall cliffs," the old

NOT FAR BELOW

trapper continued. "The walls of the canyon are gold and red and orange and rust. In some places, tall columns of rock stand like fancy pillars all along the top of the canyon."

"There are springs up there that are so hot that you can cook yer meat in them," Pa continued. "The water flows over a series of terraces, and in some places, it cools down enough so you can take a bath, if'n you want to get rid of the fleas."

"I can't wait to see it all," I said enthusiastically.

"It's something to see, all right," the old trapper said with a nod. "But Thomas, it ain't all fun and games out here." His tone was serious, so I put my carving down and gave the old trapper my full attention. "I've seen deer boiled to death in them hot springs. You ever heard an animal scream, son? It's a terrible sound. It ain't any better for the critters that scramble out of them pools. Bits and pieces of flesh drop off as they stagger away, trying to outrun the pain. I've shot more than one creature to put it out of its misery after its been burned in a hot spring. It is not a good way to die, son, so you be careful where you step."

The trapper poured himself a cup of coffee from the pot. "I'll tell you one last story and then we'll call it a night." He sat looking into the fire for a spell before he began. "Back in the early days, when I weren't much older than you, I used to trap in this area at the headwaters of the Yellowstone. There were a lot of Indians here at the time, even more then there are now, and they weren't always friendly. You had to walk cautious and keep your eyes open. I was in the forest near one of them basins full of hot springs and geysers—like this one—when I saw two Indians ahead of me, riding their ponies through the steaming pools and mud pots. They hadn't gone very far when the crust of the earth gave way under them. They plummeted out of sight, ponies and all, and a powerful lot of flame and smoke rose from the hole." He took a sip of coffee, his eyes unfocused as he saw the scene once again in his mind. "I bet hell was not far below that place," he said.

The old trapper's story sobered me. Pa had told me repeatedly that Yellowstone was a dangerous place. His hand had been scalded once in a boiling spring, and it still gave him trouble sometimes. But hearing the old trapper's stories drove the danger home in a fresh way.

"I'll be careful. I promise," I said.

The old trapper stared deep into my eyes until he was sure of my sincerity. Then he nodded and rose. "Time to hit the hay," he said. He eyed the tents and grinned at Pa.

"This sure is a fancy way to travel! Not like the old days." He disappeared inside the tent and emerged with a bedroll. "Think I'll sleep under the stars tonight," he said. "I'll mind the fire. You two get some rest."

"Thanks, Jim," Pa said gratefully. He put out his pipe, stretched, and crawled into his tent.

"Thanks for the stories," I said as I pocketed my half-finished carving and rose to my feet. "Goodnight, sir." I smiled at Jim Bridger, perhaps the most famous scout, trapper, and mountain man who ever roamed the West, and slipped into my tent.

25

Shattered

WEST YELLOWSTONE

My identical twin sister and I turned sixteen the winter our parents took us snowmobiling in Yellowstone. Our dad was an outdoors nut, so we'd practically been raised in tents. When West Yellowstone and some of the other gateway towns started featuring winter snowmobiling treks into the park, Dad was quick to take advantage.

There was an unspoken reason why Dad dragged us out of school and took us to Yellowstone. He was trying to save my twin sister, Jamie. I only hoped it wasn't too late.

What can I tell you about me and Jamie? We were both green-eyed blondes with masses of straight hair and freckled faces. Folks had trouble telling us apart when we were little, until they got to know us. Personality-wise, we were opposites. Jamie wore her hair in long braids and was into dolls and clothes and makeup. Her room was white and frilly, and she had more nail polish than the local drug store. Me, I was the tomboy. My hair was shoulder-length and tangled, and my room was decorated with plants and horse posters and baseball memorabilia. One of my life's goals was to pitch for a professional women's league. I practiced pitching all the time, summer and winter. I was pretty deadly with a snowball, if I say so myself.

Jamie and I were close despite our differences. We were the kind of twins that the science books talked about. I felt Jamie break her arm in fifth grade, and she knew I'd been in a car accident in seventh. We both felt our grandmother die in eighth grade.

When we entered high school, things changed. Jamie started hanging out with a couple of girls who were into the occult. Not good earth magic or Native American medicine. Nope. These girls used Ouija boards and called on nasty spirits and did lots of terrible things I didn't want to know about. It seemed harmless enough when we were freshmen. But as the girls' powers grew, they turned more and more toward the dark arts, and they took Jamie with them.

By the time we entered our junior year, Jamie's sunny nature had turned dark and sullen. She painted her room black and raised black widow spiders as pets. And she hung a spell mirror framed with occult symbols over her dresser. I hated that mirror. The symbols around its frame writhed whenever I looked at them. Not that I saw much of it. Jamie shut me out of her life at the beginning of the school year. And not just me—she wouldn't speak to any of us, even at meals. She hitched rides to school with her friends and didn't come home until late. Our parents' scolding fell on deaf ears. Even her teachers commented on her changed behavior.

The sixth sense that exists between twins told me that Jamie was sinking into a dark abyss from which there was no rescue. If we didn't act quickly, she would be lost to us. Feeling disloyal, I cornered Dad just before Christmas and told him everything I knew. He'd guessed some of it, but there was enough that he didn't know to make him appear rather green by the time I'd finished.

Two weeks later, our family flew to Salt Lake City and drove to West Yellowstone for a "fun family vacation" on snowmobiles. Jamie and I shared the room next door to our parents. Jamie hated sharing with me, but she wasn't given a choice. She chose the bed closest to the door and started unpacking her clothes. From the bottom of the suitcase she picked up a large, bubble-wrapped object. It was the spell mirror from her room. I bit my tongue hard to keep from shouting at her as Jamie unwrapped it lovingly and placed it on top of the dresser beside my signed baseball, which I always carried with me. Why had she brought that horrible thing?

I put my clothes away and suggested we explore the town. To my surprise, Jamie agreed. The next hour felt like old times. We poked our noses into all the shops, laughed over the funny postcards, and bought silly trinkets for one another. Our cheeks were red with cold when we got back to the hotel. Jamie lingered in the lobby, chatting with a member of the hotel staff while I rushed upstairs to heat some water in our electric coffeemaker. We'd bought packets of gourmet hot cocoa from the local grocery, and I couldn't wait to give it a try.

I was pouring a mug for Jamie when she burst into the room. She was smiling, but it wasn't her nice smile. It was the triumphant look she wore after she performed some particularly unpleasant ritual in the backwoods with her friends. "It's just as I thought. This hotel is haunted," Jamie exclaimed. "Where's my Ouija board? I must contact the spirit."

"You left your Ouija board at home," I said snappishly, handing her the mug of cocoa. She thrust it aside without drinking and sat on her bed, face dark as a thundercloud. She started cursing Mom and Dad for bringing us to Yellowstone. Then she glared at me and cursed me too. I bolted from the room in tears and went to find Mom and Dad.

We were up early the next morning and suited up for the cold ride through Yellowstone National Park. I'd been snowmobiling before, but it was Jamie's first time. She spent the morning complaining about the noise and the smell and the way the machine handled. She was too hot, she was too cold, she hated everyone and everything. I blocked out her complaints and tried to enjoy the cold fresh air on my face and the feeling of speed beneath me. The winter landscape was enthralling. Deep snow covered the ground. Pine trees loomed above the glimmering landscape. Mountains edged the huge Yellowstone caldera and the ice-encrusted lakes took my breath away. We saw otters playing at the edge of the Firehole River, and a herd of bison walked down the snow-packed surface of the road in front of us. It was amazing!

The snow had mostly melted around the hot springs in the Upper Geyser Basin, and elk were grazing among the clouds of steam. It was an enchanting wonderland. When we stopped to watch Old Faithful erupt, I thought my heart would burst.

Somewhere around Biscuit Basin, Jamie stopped complaining. There was amazement in her eyes as we watched the geyser erupt, and something else I hadn't seen in a long time. Joy. I glanced at my parents, hardly recognizable under all their snow gear. They saw it too. *Oh, please, God, help us,* I prayed. We weren't a religious family, but the simple prayer burst out of my heart. I hoped it would reach someone out there who could help my sister find her way back to us.

Over dinner, Jamie talked eagerly about all we'd seen and heard that day—the snow-encrusted bison, the lone coyote jumping headlong into a snowbank after mice. She was as eager as a kid at Christmas. But after dinner, her mood changed. I saw her talking to a local fellow who gesticulated wildly and pointed toward the roof. Jamie raced upstairs after this conversation, but I was waylaid by my dad, who wanted to play checkers. After soundly trouncing my sire three games in a row, I arrived in triumph at the door to my room and found it barred against me.

"Come on, Jamie, open up," I said, knocking loudly.

"I'm contacting the ghost," she said through the door. "Go away."

I went. Back in the lounge, I dropped disconsolately into a chair and stared blankly at the TV. The local fellow, who was working the desk that evening, came over and sat opposite me. "Boy, your sister is really into the occult," he said.

"Tell me about it," I replied despondently.

"She made me tell her every story I'd ever heard about ghosts and supernatural stuff in West Yellowstone," he continued. "Your sister was really taken with one of our local stories—it's just a rumor really—about a man who was shot by his wife when she caught him in bed with a prostitute. Nasty story, but that's the Wild West for you." He got up and stretched. "I'd better get back to the desk. Give a holler if you need anything."

I nodded my thanks and dragged myself upstairs, hoping that Jamie had finished whatever nasty occult thing she was trying. Apparently, she had. There was no barrier this time when I pushed the door open. Jamie was in bed pretending to be asleep. I saw the gleam of her eyes as I stumbled around the

SHATTERED

dark room, undressing and brushing my teeth, but she didn't speak and neither did I.

Once in bed, I cradled my signed baseball and thought about my sister. Jamie was going to get in trouble with the police if she kept walking her chosen path. And there were even worse fates than that for people who practiced black magic. But I didn't know how to stop my sister, and neither did Dad and Mom. It would take some kind of miracle, and miracles were in short supply around here.

I was awakened in the night by a wicked breeze that painfully ripped the covers off my bed. My eyes sprang open in shock, heart pounding so hard against my ribs that I thought it would leap out of my chest. An eerie light glowed from the spell mirror above the dresser. I shrieked in fear when I saw a twisted face glaring out of the glass. Tangled hair writhed around an inhuman, red-eyed face that was the source of the strange light. I looked toward Jamie's bed and yelped again. Jamie, still encased in her covers, was floating three feet above her bed! The green light emanating from the mirror surrounded her body like a net. Down our sisterly sixth sense, I could hear Jamie screaming, though no sound came from her open lips. Her eyes bulged with terror, and one hand stretched pleadingly from her covers. In my head, I heard her cry, "Save me, Jessie. Save me!"

The cold wind whirled around the room, throwing park brochures every which way, banging the closet doors, rattling the hangers. I did the only thing I could think of. I grabbed my baseball, took aim, and threw my fastball at the abomination in the mirror. The ball hit the mirror with a resounding crack, and the glass shattered. The face vanished, and with it the green light and occult wind. Jamie landed on her bed with a thump that rattled the windows. For a moment, there was stunned silence. Then Jamie started crying like a baby, and I jumped on the bed to take her in my arms.

Our parents started pounding on the adjoining door, and I got up to let them in. Jamie couldn't talk, so I told them what had happened. Mom burst into tears and hugged us both tightly. Dad was furious and frightened. He alternated between glaring at my twin and hugging her. Finally, he got up and started straightening the room. When he got to the glass-covered dresser, he stopped and stared at the remains of the spell mirror. Occult symbols writhed around the frame, and a few sharp pieces of glass clung to the edges like angry teeth. My baseball sat in the center of the mess, signature upward.

"I'll clean that up, Dad," I said firmly.

He nodded warily and picked up my bedcovers instead.

Mom and Dad took Jamie with them when they went back to their hotel room. I stayed behind to clean up the mess. I wrapped the mirror in a spare blanket without touching it and then broke it into tiny pieces. Then I found a dustpan and brush from the housekeeping closet down the hall and swept up the worst of the glass. Early the next morning, I threw the remains of the mirror away in four different dumpsters, hoping to break whatever spells still lingered by separating the pieces.

Jamie rushed to greet me with a bear hug when I came down to breakfast. When I looked into her eyes, I saw that my identical twin was back, safe and sound. The terror of the previous night had turned Jamie away from the occult forever.

I was exhausted but exhilarated that day as we explored the Canyon region on our snowmobiles, and I slept dreamlessly that night. When we left West Yellowstone at the end of the week, it was *Jamie* who begged Dad for a return trip.

As I buckled my seat belt in preparation for the flight, my foot nudged my backpack where my baseball lay. I closed my eyes and saw again a twisted green face throwing a net of power over my sister. *Oh, Jamie, that was much too close.*

Jamie bumped my elbow. I opened my eyes, and she pointed toward a cute guy across the aisle. I smiled at my twin. All was well.

Resources

"Accidentally Shot in Leg. Cooke City Prospector Engages in Scuffle with Woman for Possession of Revolver." Anaconda, MT: *Anaconda Standard*, December 17, 1903.

"An Adventure in a Geyser." Worcester, MA: *Worcester Daily Spy*, September 14, 1882.

"Annals of Wyoming." *The Wyoming History Journal*. Winter 2002, Vol. 74, No. 1. Accessed on 10/9/2012 at: www26.us.archive.org/stream/annalsofwyom74142002wyom/annalsofwyom74142002wyom_djvu.txt.

Asfar, Daniel. *Ghost Stories of Montana*. Auburn, WA: Lone Pine Publishing International, 2007.

Baumler, Ellen. *Beyond Spirit Tailings*. Helena: Montana Historical Society Press, 2005.

Beattie, Bryce A. "Ghost Stories." Bryceabeattie.com, 2011. Accessed on 10/27/2012 at www.bryceabeattie.com/2011/10/ghost-stories.

Beck, Charles B. *". . .the damned elk et my broom!": Facts, Folks and Fables of the Frontier.* Trail Lake, WY: Self-published, 1976.

Botkin, B. A., ed. *A Treasury of American Folklore*. New York: Crown, 1944.

Brunvand, Jan Harold. *The Choking Doberman and Other Urban Legends*. New York: W. W. Norton, 1984.

———. *The Vanishing Hitchhiker*. New York: W. W. Norton, 1981.

"Cinnabar, Montana Resource Brief." Accessed on 10/23/12 at www.greateryellowstonescience.org/download_product/3485/0.

Clark, Ella E. *Indian Legends from the Northern Rockies*. Norman: University of Oklahoma Press, 1966.

Clary, David A. *The Place Where Hell Bubbled Up: A History of the First National Park*. Washington, DC: Office of Publications, National Park Service, 1972.

Craughwell, Thomas A. *Urban Legends: 666 Absolutely True Stories That Happened to a Friend . . . of a Friend . . . of a Friend*. New York: Black Dog & Leventhal Publishers, 2005.

Curl, Margaret Mary. "Me." Colorado-West.com. Accessed on 10/30/2012 at http://colorado-west.com/cooke/me.pdf.

"Current Notes." Boston, MA: *Boston Journal*, September 4, 1882.

"Dashed to Pieces. Eighteen Indians and Squaws Carried Over the Falls in Yellowstone River and Dashed to Pieces." Providence, RI: *Providence Evening Press*, June 10, 1870.

Dick, David S., Douglas H. MacDonald, Steven Sheriff, and Lester E. Maas. *Cinnabar: Archaeology and History of Yellowstone's Lost Train Town.* Professional paper presented in partial fulfillment of the requirements for the degree of Master of Arts in Anthropology. Missoula: The University of Montana, 2010. Accessed on 10/23/12 at http://etd .lib.umt.edu/theses/available/etd-06182010-004451/unrestricted/ CINNABAR.pdf.

Diem, Kenneth Lee. *A Tale of Dough Gods, Bear Grease, Cantaloupe, and Sucker Oil.* Moran: University of Wyoming-National Park Service Research Center, 1986. Accessed on 10/29/2012 at: www.nps.gov/ history/history/online_books/grte/dough_gods/index.htm.

Dow, James R., Roger L. Welsch, and Susan D. Dow, eds. *Wyoming Folklore: Reminiscences, Folktales, Beliefs, Customs, and Folk Speech.* Lincoln: University of Nebraska Press, 2010.

East Fire Report. Yellowstone National Park, WY: National Park Service Department of the Interior, 2003. Accessed 9/27/2012 at: www.nps .gov/yell/parkmgmt/eastindex.htm.

Editors of *Life. The Life Treasury of American Folklore.* New York: Time Inc., 1961.

Enss, Chris. *Tales Behind the Tombstones.* Helena, MT: TwoDot, 2007.

"Fatal Explosion. Arlington Gill Killed in the Daisy Mine at Cooke City." Butte, MT: *Butte Weekly Miner,* August 20, 1896.

"Fearful Tragedy on the Yellowstone." San Francisco, CA: *San Francisco Bulletin,* June 15, 1870.

"Firefighters Now Have Fireline Between the East Fire and the Fishing Bridge Community." Yellowstone National Park, WY: Yellowstone National Park news release, August 18, 2003.

Fishbein, Seymour L. *Yellowstone Country: The Enduring Wonder.* Washington, DC: National Geographic Society, 1989.

Fitzgerald, La Verne Harriet. *Black Feather: Trapper Jim's Fables of the Sheepeater Indians in the Yellowstone.* Caldwell, ID: The Caxton Printers, Ltd., 1933.

Fifer, Barbara. *Montana Mining Ghost Towns.* Helena, MT: Farcountry Press, 2002.

Flanagan, J. T., and A. P. Hudson. *The American Folk Reader.* New York: A. S. Barnes & Co., 1958.

Foote, Stella. *Letters from "Buffalo Bill."* Billings, MT: Foote Publishing Co., 1954.

Greenway, John, comp. *Folklore of the Great West.* Palo Alto, CA: American West Publishing Company, 1969.

Grosfield, Byron. *Buckaroos and Boxcars and Selected Yarns from the Yellowstone.* Big Timber, MT: Pioneer Publishing Company, 1981.

Hagy, Alyson. *Ghosts of Wyoming*. Minneapolis, MN: Graywolf Press, 2010.

Haines, Aubrey L. *The Yellowstone Story: A History of Our First National Park: Volumes 1 & 2* (Second Revised Edition). Niwot: University Press of Colorado, 1996.

————. *Yellowstone National Park: Its Exploration and Establishment.* Washington, DC: US Department of the Interior National Park Service, 1974.

Hauck, Dennis William. *Haunted Places: The National Directory.* New York: Penguin Books, 1994.

"He Was Chased by Wolves on the Way to His Wedding." Anaconda, MT: *Anaconda Standard,* December 10, 1899.

"Historic Yellowstone Photos: Fire." WyomingTalesandTrails.com. Accessed on 9/27/2012 at www.wyomingtalesandtrails.com/yellowstone3.html.

Holub, Joan. *The Haunted States of America.* New York: Aladdin Paperbacks, 2001.

"Into a Geyser's Crater. A Tourist's Luckless Fall and Miraculous Escape from Death." Harrisburg, PA: *Patriot,* September 8, 1882.

Janetski, Joel C. *Indians in Yellowstone National Park.* Salt Lake City: The University of Utah Press, 1987.

————. *The Indians of Yellowstone Park.* Salt Lake City: The University of Utah Press, 2002.

Lankford, Andrea. *Haunted Hikes.* Santa Monica, CA: Santa Monica Press, 2006.

Larios, Shellie. *Yellowstone Ghost Stories.* Helena, MT: Riverbend Publishing, 2006.

Leach, M. *The Rainbow Book of American Folk Tales and Legends.* New York: The World Publishing Co., 1958.

Leeming, David, and Jake Pagey. *Myths, Legends, & Folktales of America.* New York: Oxford University Press, 1999.

Loendorf, Lawrence L., and Nancy Medaris Stone. *Mountain Spirit: The Sheep Eater Indians of Yellowstone.* Salt Lake City: The University of Utah Press, 2006.

"Lost in the Forest. Clyde J. Tooker Has a Rough Experience in the Woods About Cooke City." Helena, MT: *Helena Independent,* July 28, 1898.

Mattes, Merril J. *Colter's Hell & Jackson's Hole: The Fur Trappers' Exploration of the Yellowstone and Grand Teton Park Region.* Washington, DC: Yellowstone Library and Museum Association and Grand Teton Natural History Association in cooperation with National Park Service and US Department of the Interior, 1962. Accessed on 10/30/2012 at: www.nps.gov/history/history/online_books/grte1/index.htm.

Mernin, G.E. "Nez Perce at Yellowstone, 1877." NPS.gov, 2006. Accessed on 10/20/2012 at www.nps.gov/history/history/online_books/yell/nez_perce.pdf.

Moffat, Linda. *Haunted Wyoming.* Atglen, PA: Schiffer Publishing Ltd., 2011.

Munn, Debra D. *Big Sky Ghosts, Volume One.* Boulder, CO: Pruett Publishing Company, 1993.

———. *Big Sky Ghosts, Volume Two.* Boulder, CO: Pruett Publishing Company, 1994.

———. *Montana Ghost Stories.* Helena, MT: Riverbend Publishing, 2007.

———. *Wyoming Ghost Stories.* Helena, MT: Riverbend Publishing, 2008.

Murray, Earl. *Ghosts of the Old West.* Chicago: Contemporary Books, 1988.

Nabokov, Peter and Lawrence Loendorf. *Restoring a Presence: American Indians and Yellowstone National Park.* Norman: University of Oklahoma Press, 2004.

"New Life in Famous Camp. Cooke City, Where Chief Joseph Got Silver Bullets." Grand Forks, ND: *Evening Times,* October 18, 1907.

Norman, Michael, and Beth Scott. *Historic Haunted America.* New York: Tor Books, 1995.

Norris, Philetus W. *The Calumet of the Coteau, and Other Poetical Legends of the Border.* Philadelphia: J.B. Lippincott & Co., 1883.

"Over the Falls." Worcester: *Massachusetts Spy,* June 24, 1870.

Palmer, Rosemary G. *Jim Bridger: Trapper, Trader, and Guide.* Minneapolis, MN: Compass Point Books, 2007.

Raisch, Bruce A. *Haunted Hotels of the West.* Virginia Beach, VA: The Donning Company Publishers, 2009.

Rath, Robert. *Yellowstone's Hot Legends and Cool Myths.* Helena, MT: Farcountry Press, 2009.

"A Remarkable Story: A Tourist Falls into the Crater of a Geyser—Truth Stranger Than Fiction." Bozeman, MT: *Bozeman Avant Courier,* September 7, 1882.

Reevy, Tony. *Ghost Train!* Lynchburg, VA: TLC Publishing, 1998.

"Road Workers Rescued from Gas-Filled Hole." San Diego, CA: *San Diego Union,* June 27, 1939.

Roberts, Nancy. *Ghosts of the Wild West.* Columbia: University of South Carolina Press, 2008.

Rule, Leslie. *Coast to Coast Ghosts.* Kansas City, KS: Andrews McMeel Publishing, 2001.

Saunders, Richard L., ed. *A Yellowstone Reader.* Salt Lake City: The University of Utah Press, 2003.

Schlosser, S. E. "Dark Presence." Story collected by author in an interview with Cody resident (A. W.) at Cody Cowboy Village on 9/8/2012.

———. "Fire!" Author's experience at Nine-Mile Trailhead on 9/6/2012.

———. "Floating above the Bed." Story collected by author in an interview with U. F., currently living in Saint Augustine, Florida. January 2009.

———. "Hello, Darlin'." Author's experience at Irma Hotel in Cody on evening of 9/7/2012.

———. "I Want to Go Home." Author's experience at Lake Hotel on evening of 8/31/2012 and morning of 9/1/2012.

———. "The Sentinel." Story collected by the author in an interview with Yellowstone tourist D. H. on 8/26/2012.

Schullery, Paul, and Sarah Stevenson, eds. *People and Place: The Human Experience in Greater Yellowstone.* Yellowstone National Park, WY: Proceedings of the Fourth Biennial Conference on the Greater Yellowstone Ecosystem, October 12–15, 1997.

"Second Degree Verdict Given Against Boden: Old Prospector Convicted of Killing Mrs. Miller and His Punishment Is Left to Court. Four Ballots Taken." Anaconda, MT: *Anaconda Standard,* January 12, 1922.

Skinner, Charles M. *American Myths and Legends,* Vol. 1. Philadelphia: J. B. Lippincott, 1903.

———. *Myths and Legends of Our Own Land,* Vols. 1 & 2. Philadelphia: J. B. Lippincott, 1896.

"Sly Mouse Is Yellowstone Hotel Ghost." Rockford, IL: *Daily Register Gazette,* June 20, 1928.

"Sly Mouse Ghost of Park Hotel." Davenport, IA: *Davenport Iowa Democrat and Leader,* June 13, 1928.

Smith, Barbara. *Ghost Stories of the Rocky Mountains.* Vol. 1. Auburn, WA: Lone Pine Publishing, 1999.

———. *Ghost Stories of the Rocky Mountains.* Vol. 2. Auburn, WA: Ghost House Books, 2003.

Spence, Lewis. *North American Indians: Myths and Legends Series.* London: Bracken Books, 1985.

Stark, Mike. "E.C. Waters Left to Rot in Yellowstone National Park." Billings, MT: *Billings Gazette,* July 16, 2007. Accessed on 10/25/2012 at: http://billingsgazette.com/news/state-and-regional/wyoming/article_1e5b84e8-8cf4-5505-857b-bfdd9cfe070b.html.

Stevens, Karen. *Haunted Montana.* Helena, MT: Riverbend Publishing, 2007.

Students of Haskell Institute. *Myths, Legends, Superstitions of North American Indian Tribes.* Cherokee, NC: Cherokee Publications, 1995.

Swagerty, William R. "Chief Joseph and the Nez Perce Indians." Stockton, CA: University of the Pacific, 2005. Accessed on 10/28/2012 at: www.windriverhistory.org/exhibits/chiefjoseph/chiefjoseph01.htm.

"Tells How He Killed Woman and Buried Body: His Night of Horror: Aged Prospector Occupies Witness Stand Entire Day." Anaconda, MT: *Anaconda Standard,* January 10, 1922.

"Tragedy in Yellowstone Park. Mrs. Trischman, Who Recently Attempted Suicide, Murders One of Her Children." Butte, MT: *Butte Weekly Miner.* Vol. XX, issue 23, p. 15, June 8, 1899.

Turner, Erin H. *It Happened in Yellowstone.* Guilford, CT: Globe Pequot Press, 2012.

"A Visit from a Bear. An Old Monster Invaded a Yellowstone Park Hotel." Trenton, NJ: *Trenton Evening Times,* June 19, 1900.

Walter, Dave. *Montana Campfire Tales.* Helena, MT: TwoDot, 1997.

———. *More Montana Campfire Tales.* Helena, MT: Farcountry Press, 2002.

Whealdon, Bon I., et al. *I Will Be Meat for My Salish.* Helena: Montana Historical Society Press, 2001.

Watry, Elizabeth A., and Lee H. Whittlesey. *Images of America: Fort Yellowstone.* Charleston, SC: Arcadia Publishing, 2012.

"Weather Tames East Fire in Yellowstone." Billings, MT: *Billings Gazette,* August 18, 2003.

"West Yellowstone, Montana Ghost Sightings." Ghostsofamerica.com. Accessed on 10/9/2012 at www.ghostsofamerica.com/5/Montana_West_Yellowstone_ghost_sightings.html.

"Wife Says Sargent Was An Innocent Man." New York: *New York Times,* August 17, 1913.

"Yellowstone, Montana; Territory; Attempted; Eighteen; Death." New Orleans: *Times-Picayune,* June 5, 1870.

Whittlesey, Lee H. *Death in Yellowstone: Accidents and Foolhardiness in the First National Park.* Lanham, MD: Roberts Rinehart Publishers, 1995.

———. *Storytelling in Yellowstone: Horse and Buggy Tour Guides.* Albuquerque: University of New Mexico Press, 2007.

Whittlesey, Lee H., ed. *Lost in the Yellowstone.* Salt Lake City: University of Utah Press, 1995.

"Wildlife Hydrothermal Hazards." NPS.gov. Accessed on 10/16/2012 at www.nps.gov/yell/ofvec/exhibits/ecology/wildlife/hazards3.htm.

About the Author

Author S. E. Schlosser has been telling stories since she was a child, when games of "let's pretend" quickly built themselves into full-length stories. A graduate of the Institute of Children's Literature and Rutgers University, she also created and maintains www.AmericanFolklore.net, where she shares a wealth of stories from all fifty states, some dating back to the origins of America.

About the Illustrator

Artist Paul Hoffman trained in painting and printmaking. His first extensive illustration work on assignment was in Egypt, drawing ancient wall reliefs for the University of Chicago. His work graces books of many genres—including children's titles, textbooks, short story collections, natural history volumes, and numerous cookbooks. For *Spooky Yellowstone*, he employed a scratchboard technique and an active imagination.